PASS IT ON

How to Make Your Own Family Keepsakes

MARGUERITE ASHWORTH BRUNNER

SOVEREIGN BOOKS
New York

Designed by Irving Perkins

Library of Congress Cataloging in Publication Data
Brunner, Marguerite Ashworth.
  Pass it on, how to make your own family keepsakes.
  Includes index.
  1. Handicraft.   2. Heirlooms.   I. Title.
TT157.B792   745.5   78-10294
ISBN 0-671-18377-X
ISBN 0-671-18376-1 (paper)

To my mother, Addie Caviness Ashworth,
who lovingly taught me many things

Contents

Introduction   3
1 A Record of Our Times   7
2 Collect Valuable Autographs   12
3 Compile Your Personal Cookbook   16
4 Trace Your Family Tree   26
5 Unusual Easy-to-Make Quilts   31
6 Coverlets   38
7 Samplers   47
8 Braiding   50
9 Pressed Flowers   54
10 The Art of Drying Flowers   62
11 Decoupage   65
12 Potichomania: Gluing Paper Cutouts to Glass   73
13 Velvet Painting and Appliqués   76
14 Painting on Wood   79
15 Wood Whittling   83
16 Dollhouses and Miniature Doll Furniture   89
17 Heirloom Dolls to Make   100
18 Treasured Egg-Crafted Heirlooms   109
19 Dough Items   115
20 Handmade Christmas Tree Ornaments   118
21 Shadow-Box or Frame Your Treasures   127
22 Crafts for Children   130
23 Where to Sell Your Crafts and Buy Supplies   139
   Index   151

PASS IT ON

*How to Make Your Own
Family Keepsakes*

Introduction

ONE morning a well-dressed, mildde-aged woman walked into my antiques shop in North Carolina and asked me to show her some heirlooms—things suitable to pass down to her children when she died. I was stunned. When you're in business you hear a lot of strange requests, but this one topped them all. She was obviously well-to-do and I was eager to sell her something, so I asked whether she had anything particular in mind.

She seemed a little embarrassed. "I never gave it much thought until this morning," she said, "but I've just come from a friend's funeral, and everywhere I turned, I heard people talking about all the beautiful heirlooms she was leaving to her children. I have three grown children of my own, and it made me realize that I haven't a single one to leave to them."

If it hadn't been so tragic, I'd have laughed out loud. I was reminded of the Pittsburgh woman who once bought a beautiful painting of an old-fashioned girl from me, saying, "I'll tell my friends it's my grandmother!"

The dictionary defines an heirloom as a personal chattel, which by its connection with an estate descends to an heir. You cannot buy someone else's heirloom and claim it as your own, for there can be no sentiment attached to the treasures of another.

The heirlooms most treasured in our times are those into which loving thought was woven—the handmade quilts and bedspreads our grandmothers worked over tediously by lamplight; the hand-hewed toys and utensils our grandfathers made to fill the needs of the families they loved and cared for; the jewels designed especially for a loved one;

3

the paintings of our own ancestors, not of unknown faces we pretend are our kin.

At this point, it seems fitting to tell you of an experience of mine that points out how deeply heirlooms can affect our feelings.

A very good customer asked me to travel to a small Virginia town to help her catalog her mother's possessions. "I swore I'd never set foot in that house again after mother married that no-good Charlie," she said. "I always thought he married her for her money and the security of a home, and I hated him for it. But now he's died—and he had the gall to name me beneficiary of my own mother's things! Of course I don't want them, but I must dispose of them so the house can be sold." She asked me to come and help arrange for an auction. She assured me that I could have first choice of things I wanted for my shop, so I eagerly agreed.

From everything she had told me, I expected to find a run-down old house, showing years of neglect, but it didn't turn out that way. When we got there, I was shocked to see it freshly painted in glossy white, with bright green shutters and window boxes heady with a wild array of colorful petunias. The flower beds in the yard bloomed with a pro-fusion of color—it looked like something out of a magazine.

My friend was obviously surprised, too. Her lawyer, who was there waiting for us, said that Charlie had painted it himself. "He wanted the house to be as beautiful as it had always been—he loved it the same way your mother did."

Inside the big hall, my friend said, "Nothing's changed! It's just the way I remember it!" The grandfather clock was still ticking away, and she traced her fingers through the dust on a half-moon mahogany table that held a silver card tray. "I'll bet that tray never held a calling card after mother married Charlie!" my friend said.

In the dining room, all the china and silver had been placed on the table and sideboard. In the corner, on a teacart, was her mother's Dresden tea set. I was filled with excitement—these were the kinds of treasures every antiques dealer dreams of, and I felt sure my friend would not charge me exorbitant prices for any of them.

"I can still see my mother pouring tea into these fragile cups," she said, "and still hear her telling how she brought them back from her honeymoon wrapped in her soft cotton underwear, and not a single piece was broken. Hearing that story over and over again was the price you paid for drinking tea from her cups—for as day follows night, they went together."

The floorboards squeaked under our weight, and I couldn't help feeling sorry for the old house. It has always seemed strange to me the way houses have such definite personalities, but I think they do. I was sure this had been a happy house and it was sad there was no one left to love it.

As I took out my notebook and began listing the china and silver pieces, my friend sat down in an old walnut rocker that squeaked as loudly as the floor. "It's going to rain," she said.

The lawyer laughed. "There's not a cloud in the sky and I heard the forecast—no rain today."

"I don't care," said my friend. "My grandfather made this rocker so my grandmother could rock my mother when she was a baby, and it always squeaked when it was going to rain. My mother used to say it had rheumatism and didn't like being rocked in bad weather, and she never allowed anyone to sit on it then."

I sensed a strange mood coming over my friend. She moved a pile of neatly stacked patterned quilts from the sofa and put them on a straight chair. "Do you think," she asked thoughtfully, "that when you sell that rocker you can tell the new owner it's a fair-weather chair?"

I told her she sounded like a mother putting up her children for adoption. For, after all, we antiques dealers don't always know about the people who buy our wares.

Well, to make a long story short, I will simply say that it did rain that afternoon—a sudden shower that seemed to come from nowhere—and my friend changed right before my eyes from the hate-filled woman who had come to the house to one filled with compassion. I know she regretted the years she'd stayed away. I believe she forgave her mother for marrying—even softened her feelings for Charlie. It was with some embarrassment that she asked me to stop listing things, for she simply couldn't part with one of them. In fact, two years later she moved back into that old house, and I suspect that the teatime story is still being told and that a certain rocker is never sat on when it rains.

Today, with the hustle and bustle of our busy lives, we are forgetting how to make our own heirlooms. We may well be cheating our children of their rightful heritage by not taking the time to create the loving, thoughtful links between our generation and theirs.

We live in historical times; yet our children and their children may read about them only from their textbooks. Too few of us are preserving our own small corner of history for those who come after us. I recently saw a Civil War scrapbook bring over a hundred dollars at a country auction. It held letters, mementoes, clippings and one family's account of how that dreadful war had touched their lives. This was an heirloom

5

—collected and preserved for generations to come. A patchwork quilt, handmade with dated squares, also brought more than a hundred dollars, despite the fact that it was faded and worn.

How often, after a flood or fire, have we heard people lament that they could replace their furnishings but not their heirlooms? The things we treasure most don't always cost the most money. When we lose an heirloom, we may well tell the insurance company that it had little monetary value, but the sentimental value was beyond estimation. It is this sentimental value that marks the true heirloom—warm things that seem to radiate love and thoughtfulness and bring back memories. Things that have passed down through our families, like a continuous chain, binding us to the past and our ancestors. In the same way, we ourselves, can make so many things that will pass down and become heirlooms with inestimable value for our own children. By so doing, we'll be weaving our own chains between our time and the future. That is what this book is all about.

1

A Record of Our Times

WHEN I pass a pile of newspapers out on the curb, I often wonder if anybody bothered to glean a little bit of "history-in-the-making" from their pages before discarding them.

Headlines like these: *Kennedy Assassinated, President Johnson Dead, Nixon Resigns*—they capture truly historical moments and should be preserved for our children. Twenty years from now a scrapbook on President Nixon's near-impeachment will be more valuable than many jewels. In fact, thousands of requests for newspapers with the headline *Nixon Resigns* poured into the *Washington Post* in the weeks following his resignation, but the edition sold out immediately, and buyers were soon paying as much as $10 a copy—when they could find one. Within a few short weeks that headline had become a collector's item, and this was true for newspapers all over the country.

In Washington, the *Star-News* ran an article telling readers how to preserve their own Nixon resignation headline. They described it as "the headline for ages, set in the largest type size (184-point) in our 122-year history. How best to preserve such a dramatic front page, other than just stowing it away? "Cool it," they said. "Simply cool the hot page."

They explained that an untreated paper stored at room temperature away from light would last fewer than fifty years, but for each ten degrees the temperature is lowered, the life of the paper is roughly doubled. So, said the *Star-News*, "if you're interested in preservation, in pristine condition, for five hundred years, when it might be worth a great deal more, look to the freezer."

They suggested two methods for treating the newsprint in order to preserve it—but it's important not to treat any paper that's less than six months old. It takes that long for the ink to dry. So here's what you do, before you start making your newspaper heirlooms:

Storing Your Papers Until the Ink Dries

A heavy cardboard storage chest, designed to slide under the bed and which may be purchased from almost any drugstore or department store, is ideal for storing your papers during this time, or until you're ready to use them. These chests are particularly good because you'll be able to store the papers flat. Remember to store them in a cool place, preferably an unheated room or the basement of your house. If you decide to use other types of boxes (not air-tight), put some mothballs in to discourage the various bugs that love to make a feast on paper.

Treating Newsprint to Make It Last

When the ink is dry, you can treat your papers in one of these two ways suggested by the *Star-News*. The first method requires a bit of skill.

1. Find a siphon bottle, the kind used to serve carbonated water. A cartridge of carbon dioxide comes with it.
2. Buy 10 grams of light magnesium carbonate from your local druggist.
3. Mix the magnesium carbonate with cold water and pour into the siphon bottle.
4. Attach the cartridge and spray the contents into a stainless steel tray large enough to hold the page. Soak the page for about one hour.
5. Remove the page carefully and place it on a screen to dry.

Here's the second method, suggested by the director of technical services at the National Archives:

Simply place a tablet of milk of magnesia in a quart bottle of club soda and let it chill overnight in the refrigerator. Then soak the page with this mixture, removing it carefully for drying.

When your treated papers are dry again, now is the time to be creative—let your imagination run wild. Remember it isn't just saving the paper that counts, it's your individual, personal touch that changes the ordinary into a real heirloom. Think ahead. Take into consideration how much space your family will have for storing things. If quarters are cramped, you'll naturally be creating smaller things.

There are many ways to use and preserve news stories. Here are a few of mine, though I'm sure you'll think of many of your own.

KEEP A NEWS SCRAP BOOK

In my own big scrapbook, I've preserved all the big Nixon news stories from the 1968 election through Watergate and his resignation. A professor friend of mine is keeping a scrapbook on the Kennedy family, beginning with Jack Kennedy's inauguration, covering the assassinations of Jack and Bobby, and now being filled with clippings on Ted. Another friend keeps one filled with political cartoons since the Roosevelt days.

The Bicentennial news stories, mementoes, souvenirs, and programs will also become quite valuable as time goes by. If you've been foresighted enough to keep them, put them into a scrapbook. Remember that souvenirs from expositions and world's fairs of years past bring high prices at auctions. Your own Bicentennial mementoes and news clippings will become treasures, too.

Scrapbook possibilities are unlimited, and yours may cover one subject or a wide range—in any event, it's bound to become more and more valuable with time.

Newspaper-size scrapbooks can be found in stationery stores everywhere. They come in two sizes: 25-by-19⅞ inches or 24½-by-19½ inches. They have heavy cardboard covers and fifty pages of heavy paper inside. Refills are available, too.

MAKE A NEWSPRINT LAMPSHADE

Old, unattractive shades become conversation pieces when covered with headlines. Here's how to do it.

1. Carefully cut your newspaper to fit the individual sides of your shade, or else cut them so headlines make a sort of all-over patchwork.
2. Use a water-soluble decoupage glue (such as Elmer's or other white glue), and apply as directed to paper and frame.
3. Carefully place your newspaper as you want it, and smooth it on so it adheres closely without air bubbles.
4. Allow to dry thoroughly, for at least twenty-four hours.
5. Apply a clear varnish or shellac and let dry before using.

9

PASS IT ON

Make a Newsprint Tray

If you have an old metal tray that's somewhat worn, and doesn't look like much, you can rejuvenate it with newsprint. In fact, sets of snack trays become interesting and valuable when decorated this way.

1. Cut your newspapers to fit the bottom of the tray.
2. Apply a cement glue—the kind used in model airplane kits. (You can't use water-soluble glue for this; you need cement glue on metal.)
3, 4, 5. Same as for Newsprint Lampshade, above.

Line Old Trunks or Boxes with Newsprint

Lining old trunks with newspapers is not a new idea. In olden days, newspapers were not discarded as readily as they are today. After being passed around, often from family to family, they were frequently used to line boxes, wrap things in, or even to wallpaper rooms. My idea is to select special newspaper topics for your linings. A trunk lined with news accounts of births, marriages, and accomplishments of members of your family, or of their special interests, would make an exceptional wedding gift for one of your children, and an heirloom they'll be happy to pass on. Here's how to do it.

Preparing the Trunk

1. Make sure the inside of the trunk is smooth, clean and dry. It may be necessary to scrape off any old lining, if it's lumpy or torn in places.
2. Use fine sandpaper and go over the surface even if it's in good shape, for sanding will make the glue adhere better.

Arranging the Clippings

Do not start gluing until you have enough clippings to cover the surfaces. If there are only a few clippings, but you would like to start your trunk anyway, do just the lid. Decide how to arrange the clippings on the entire surface. If you're doing a side, lay out a paper (newspaper will do) the exact size of the surface to be covered, and mark your clipping layout on it before beginning the gluing.

Gluing

Again, use water-soluble glue. (Elmer's is excellent.)

1. Glue clippings one by one, in the order in which you'll apply them.

10

2. Put each clipping in place, smoothing it on with a paint roller or similar roller so that all bubbles and lumps of glue are evenly rolled out.
3. Let dry for 24 hours.
4. Apply clear varnish or shellac. (Spray cans are desirable on such surfaces.) Apply four or five coats, making sure that each coat is completely dry before applying the next.

FRAME THE FRONT PAGE

You can frame the entire front page of a newspaper with historical headlines to hang on the wall of your den or study. Use a plain or carved frame, as you like. A series of them, covering the presidential elections during your lifetime, would make an interesting wall. An Army officer friend of mine frames war headlines. His collection begins with the end of World War I and covers historic headlines to the present date.

If you haven't yet saved any historic headlines, don't despair—history is continually in the making, and it's never too late to begin framing your own record of our time.

SAVE THE ENTIRE PAPER

A young mother I know saved the complete newspaper of the day each of her children was born. She zips up the paper in a plastic bag, along with the child's birth certificate. "When the children are older," my friend says, "they'll be interested in what happened in the world on the day they were born. When they reach an age to appreciate it, I'll present them with their paper as a birthday gift."

One last point: If you have a large family, you must think about preserving a little bit of history-in-the-making for each child. I've seen some terrible squabbles when there was only a single family photograph album or Bible to share among several children. Earmark your creations early for each of your children, letting them know that you're making certain things especially for them. They will love you for it, and you'll be able to see the pride and affection that grow with your thoughtfulness.

11

2

Collect Valuable Autographs

ON a recent Washington talk show, an interesting woman told how she began her hobby of autograph collecting. Over the past twenty years she has collected over a thousand letters and cards signed by famous people from all over the world. She has cards from kings and queens, presidents, diplomats, senators, congressmen, and all the famous people from the entertainment world. This is how she began and still goes on.

After Christmas each year, she buys her next year's Christmas cards when they're on sale at half price. Then, during the year, she usually addresses about five hundred of them to famous people all over the world. Inside the card she writes: "May I please have one of your lovely Christmas cards this year? With your personal autograph?" Then she signs her name, adding her address below her signature.

She warns that although she asks for personal signatures, it is possible that some cards may be sent out with stamped signatures done by secretaries or someone else. If you observe closely you can tell the difference between a pen and ink lettered signature and a stamped one. An original will be less perfect—ink may be heavier in places. But a card from a celebrity, even if the signature is stamped, has a value to collectors as a whole, if not as an autograph alone.

It is good when the collector actually sees the celebrity sign a program or card in their presence. This way there is no doubt that the autograph is authentic and original. Other signatures often have to be checked by an expert to authenticate that they are originals.

The first time, she received only fifty-four cards in return—but among them was one from a queen, a president, and many other notables. She was so excited with the results that since then she's been sending out her cards in September and October, giving the recipients plenty of time to add her name to their mailing lists.

"Never give up!" she says. "If you don't receive a reply the first or second year, remember that your card may have been misaddressed and may have gone astray in the mail." Sometimes they have to be forwarded, which delays them, too. If, however, after the second year you've had no response and you've made sure the address is correct (she contacts the various embassies for addresses of foreign notables), try a new tactic. If you see news items about these people during the year, save them and enclose one or two with your card the third year. She finds this a good way to get the personal attention of people whose autographs she seeks.

She advises collectors to keep a diary, listing the names of those to whom they've sent cards, along with the message and a record of responses.

You can also do this for your friends. For instance, several years ago I heard that Lawrence Welk has one of the largest Christmas card lists in the country—he sends them to anybody who asks. As I have a dear friend who's a Welk fan, I sent along her name and address, and now she receives a beautiful card from him each year.

You can get greetings for other occasions, too. Most of our recent First Ladies have sent cards just for the asking with birthday greetings for elderly people, or congratulations for fiftieth wedding anniversaries and other such special celebrations. You get these by writing to the First Lady's Secretary at the White House, Washington, DC 20500.

While many public figures will send you their autograph simply for the asking, I think the most valuable are those at the end of a personal letter. I have many that I prize, although I never started out with the intention of collecting them. Some came in response to articles I had written as a newspaper reporter. My most treasured are those from Bobby and Jack Kennedy. I've corresponded with authors of books I've enjoyed—and even got to meet and become friends with some of them. Then, too, as a fund-raiser for various political campaigns, I've received letters of gratitude from many of our political leaders.

Letters from politicians are always worth collecting. For instance, an early letter from Nelson Rockefeller became much more valuable when he was named Vice President. This holds true of any of our representatives or senators. If you're serious about collecting political autographs,

13

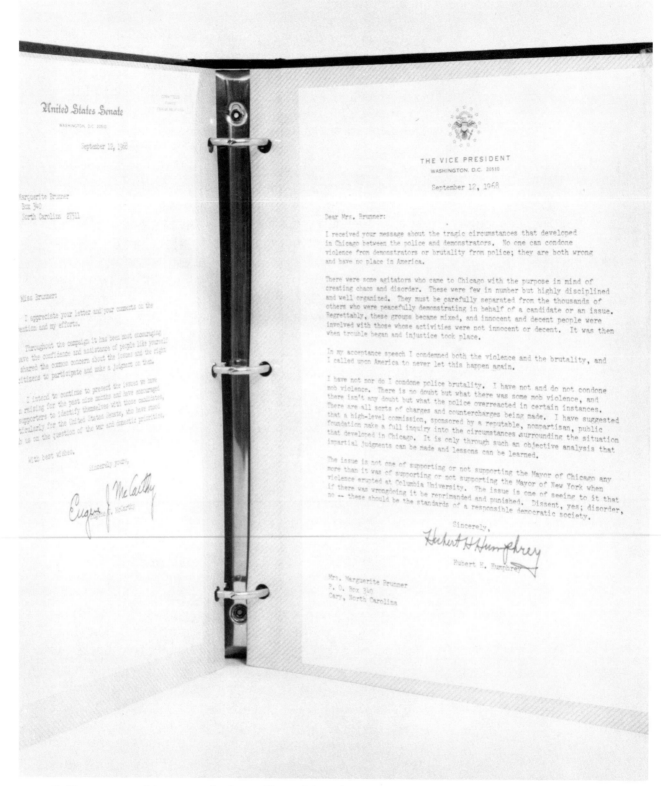

Letters preserved in magnetic photo album. *Photo by Ross Chapple*

14

in coming elections write to your preferred candidates for governor, congressman or President. Offer to work for them or otherwise further their cause. Ask personal questions, so your letters stand out from the perfunctory kind that can be answered with form letters. Make yours one that requires personal attention, and you'll probably get it.

On the other hand, you never know what response you'll receive when you write to strangers. I remember when my daughters gave me a lovely little book, *As a Man Thinketh* by James Allen. I enjoyed it so much that I wrote to the author in England and told him so. Imagine my embarrassment when his daughter answered, telling me her father had passed away years before. As I say, you never know what your letters may bring in return, but it does make life interesting.

Preserving your autographs is as important as collecting them. Never glue them into a book. Buy one of the magnetic photo albums with clear plastic pages that lift up so you can insert your letters in place. One way to make your album more interesting is to place a copy of your own letter opposite the answer, so people can view them together as a real correspondence. Your family will cherish it even more for the record of your own personal participation in the events of our time.

3

Compile Your Personal Cookbook

REMEMBER the excitement of coming across one of your grand-mother's old recipes tucked away in one of her books or in the family Bible? How you couldn't wait to try it out? Or how it took you years and years to pry a secret family recipe from your best friend for that heavenly stew of hers your husband always raves about? All of us have pet recipes like these—and what an heirloom a compilation of these rare treasures would be for our children or some young cook coming after us.

Many delectable recipes were never written down; they passed on with their authors. There were many good cooks who guarded their recipes so secretly that they didn't even trust them to their relatives. Then again, many outstanding cooks kept their best recipes "in their heads," and passed them down verbally from one generation to another.

If you've ever bought a box of Sophie Mae's Peanut Brittle, you've probably read about how this famous recipe was almost lost. They tell us that in 1866, Sophie Mae Hall, a gracious Southern lady widowed by the Civil War, was desperately searching for a way to support her three children. She had always been complimented on the candy she made for fun, so she salvaged her recipes and began offering "Choice Home Made Candies in Small Quantities" for sale. Soon, the fame of her rich, crackly peanut brittle spread through many Georgia counties. For some fifteen years, through the difficult time of Reconstruction, Sophie Mae supported her family by selling her candy. Then in 1912, while browsing through some old family documents, Sophie Mae's granddaughter (and namesake) came across the original recipe. Time had faded the ink, but not the fine ingredients and the delectable flavor. Once again, Sophie Mae's Peanut Brittle was made according to the traditional recipe—without a trace of imitation flavoring or coloring. Suppose that the first Sophie Mae had not written down the recipe? It might have been lost forever.

I hope I've convinced you to write down your own. Before giving you some recipes to start with, I'll tell you how I make my own cookbook to hold them. The best book to house your culinary treasures is the largest school notebook (at least one hundred pages) you can find. Never use a loose-leaf book, because people always borrow pages from those. Then, too, as years pass, pages tear loose.

If you want to make a special cookbook as a wedding gift or gift for a friend or member of your family, you may re-cover the cardboard binding with material. Glue the fabric with Elmer's or rubber cement onto the outside, folding it over the edges to the other side of the binding. Then cut out magazine pictures and glue them on the inside to cover the rough edges.

I like to write my recipes in longhand. A hand-written book is more personal and also more valuable than a printed one.

Now to start you off with recipes, let me tell you about Elizabeth Husch. When she and her family left Hungary in 1947 for a refugee camp in Austria, Mrs. Husch carried in her head the recipe for her mother's famous apple strudel—she relied completely on memory and never wrote it down.

Four years later, the Husch family came to Maryland to work on a farm in exchange for food and housing. The pastor of their church taught the family English, and in appreciation, Mrs. Husch began making her apple strudel for church bazaars. It was an immediate success and always sold out as fast as she could make it—people drove for miles just to buy her strudel. Everyone wanted the recipe, and, finally, Mrs. Husch wrote it down for them. With a little practice, she said, anyone could learn to stretch the dough thin enough to make perfect strudel. "Don't worry," she told them, "if holes form while stretching the dough. When the strudel is rolled up, the holes won't be seen." (Anyway, you can use some of the extra dough for patching, if needed.)

I found making this strudel an all-day job, but it's worth it; I've never tasted anything more delicious. So I'm passing it on to you, and I'm sure it will be a favorite in your own "homemade" cookbook.

17

Covered notebook for cookbook, with quilted pocket.

18

Inside of prepared cookbook. *Photo by Ross Chapple*

19

ELIZABETH HUSCH'S APPLE STRUDEL
SERVES 20

10 pounds of cooking apples
Juice of 4 lemons

Dough
7½ cups self-rising flour
2 eggs
2 teaspoons salt
2⅓ cups warm water, mixed with
2 teaspoons white vinegar
2 tablespoons sweet butter,
melted

Sour Cream Sauce
1 quart sour cream
½ cup sugar

4 eggs, separated
2 teaspoons vanilla extract
Juice of 2 lemons

Rest of the Filling
½ pound butter (2 sticks),
melted
1½ cups bread crumbs
¾ cup golden raisins
¼ teaspoon ground nutmeg
¼ teaspoon ground cloves
1½ teaspoons cinnamon
Confectioner's sugar

Preheat the oven to 350 degrees.

First peel, core, and slice the apples. Sprinkle with lemon juice and set aside.

To make the dough, put flour in a large bowl and make a well in the center. Into the well place 2 eggs, salt, and warm water/vinegar mixture. Mix well with hands. Add the melted butter and knead vigorously for five minutes or until dough does not stick to the fingers or bowl. Cut into three equal parts. Place on a lightly floured heavy linen cloth, card-table size. Cover with a clean kitchen towel and let rest 10 to 15 minutes.

While the dough rests, prepare the sauce and the rest of the filling.

For the sauce: Mix sour cream, sugar, 4 egg yolks, vanilla extract, and lemon juice. In a separate bowl, beat the egg whites until soft peaks form, then sprinkle in 1 tablespoon sugar. Continue beating whites until stiff. Fold whites into sour cream mixture and set aside.

For the rest of the filling: Melt the butter very gently, then pour it into a small pitcher or measuring cup with a lip and keep warm. You'll have about 1 cup. Measure the bread crumbs into a small bowl and keep them separate. In another bowl, mix together the raisins, nutmeg, cloves, and cinnamon. Set aside.

Now you're ready to get back to the dough: Flour your hands and take one piece of the dough (leave the other two pieces covered).

Gently pat your piece of dough on the floured cloth and roll it out into a 10-inch round.

Pour 2 tablespoons of warm, melted butter into the center of the round—use a pastry brush to brush the butter evenly over the surface. Then start stretching the dough thin, as you go. Don't pull with the fingers or you'll tear it; work with the flat tops of your hands from knuckles to wrist—you'll see how nicely the dough circle will enlarge as you stretch it around. Keep stretching until it's very thin and transparent, and don't worry if it hangs over the edges of the table.

Remove any thick portions of dough around the edges by holding down dough with the left hand while tearing with the right hand, winding the excess dough around the hand as you go. (Mrs. Husch uses this leftover dough for dumplings.)

Now you start filling: Take ⅓ of the apple slices and spread them over the entire surface of dough, leaving a 1-inch margin around the edges. Drop 1 cup of the Sour Cream Sauce by spoonfuls over the apple slices. Then sprinkle on ½ cup of your bread crumbs. Take ⅓ of your raisin filling and sprinkle evenly over all.

Sprinkle a little of the melted butter around edges of dough. Quickly overlap margin on all sides of dough over filling. Sprinkle overlap with a little more melted butter. Take edge of cloth and roll dough away from you until strudel is rolled up like a jelly roll. Cut in half, and gently place the two halves in a greased baking pan, side by side. Sprinkle a little of the melted butter where the two rolls touch. (So far you'll have used ⅓-cup of melted butter—about 5 tablespoons in all.)

Repeat the process with the two remaining pieces of dough, apples, sauce, and the rest of the filling. When the 6 strudel rolls are all placed in your baking dish, pour the remaining 3 cups of Sour Cream Sauce evenly over them just before baking.

Put into a preheated 350-degree oven and bake for one hour. The strudel should be nicely browned on top. Cool slightly and dust confectioner's sugar over the top.

The strudel can be frozen after baking and cooling.

I grew up during the Depression, when we had to make do with what we had, and I've accumulated some "poor-times" recipes that could laugh inflation right out of existence. They are in my cookbook, for we never know when hard times may come upon us again—but also because they taste so good.

Nothing went to waste in those days. Celery tops and spring onion tops were slowly parched in a low oven or left to dry on a sunny window sill. Crumbled up, they went into a jar for soups and stews. Leftover vegetables of all sorts were dumped into a single jar and placed alongside the ice in our old icebox to be added to potatoes, onions, canned tomatoes, and a can of corned beef.

Many times, during those lean years, I saw my mother feed ten or more hungry youngsters after a high school football game with that single can of corned beef and a few leftovers. To increase the stew, Mother simply added more potatoes and onions. The corned beef broke into a million little pieces and seasoned the whole pot, lending a delicious flavor to the stew. There was always enough, no matter how many extra kids we brought home with us, and everybody loved it.

Her hot breads and "football stew" were favorites we clamored for, and fortunately for me, my mother compiled her own cookbook—one she copied over for me, and I treasure it above all my possessions.

All cooks have special recipes their families enjoy, and most of us are noted for some special dish. Every time there's a picnic, I'm asked to bring potato salad, for my mother taught me a secret about making it. I always mix the ingredients while the potatoes are hot—that way the onion and celery flavors permeate the potatoes and make the salad special. In my mother's cookbook, there are lots of tips that change ordinary foods into something special. A tart apple added to tuna-fish salad does wonders. It's secrets like these that make our homemade cookbooks heirlooms to be treasured forever.

Every Christmas I receive phone calls from friends and strangers asking for my Kentucky Whiskey Cake recipe. (That's also my mother's.) It seems that everyone who tastes it asks for the recipe, and, because it is such a holiday favorite, I often bake little ones (in Planter's small nut cans) and send them as gifts in lieu of cards. For regular-size cakes, I find that one-pound nut or coffee cans make ideal baking pans. Here's how I make it:

KENTUCKY WHISKEY CAKE
MAKES 10–12 COFFEE-CAN CAKES

1 pound candied red cherries (cut them in half)
1½ cups (½ pound) white raisins
1 pint bourbon whiskey
2¼ cups white sugar
1 cup brown sugar
¾ pound butter or margarine
6 egg yolks
5 cups sifted flour (always sift before measuring)
2 teaspoons nutmeg
1 teaspoon baking powder
6 egg whites
1 pound (4 cups) shelled pecans, broken up

22

Preheat the oven to 250 degrees.

Soak the cherries and raisins in the whiskey overnight. (Use a covered china or glass bowl—not metal.)

Cream sugar (both brown and white) and butter until light and fluffy. Add egg yolks and beat well. Add the soaked fruit and its remaining liquor. Reserve a small portion of flour for the nuts. Sift the remaining flour with nutmeg and baking powder and add to the fruit and butter mixture.

Beat the egg whites until they stand in peaks, then fold them into the batter. Mix the nuts with the small portion of reserved flour, and add them last, distributing them through the batter.

Take 10 or 12 1-pound nut or coffee cans and cut out brown paper to make linings for bottoms and sides. (Use paper bags for this.) Lightly butter the linings before inserting them. Fold in the batter to an inch below the top—the cake is heavy and does not rise very much in baking pans. Put into a preheated oven and bake at 250 degrees for 3 to 4 hours, or until done—when a fork inserted in center comes out clean.

These cakes can be made weeks in advance, wrapped in foil and frozen until ready for use.

If you have several children, make a cookbook for each of them. To make it strictly a family book, you should write notes of interest around each recipe: "This is Uncle John's favorite," or "Grandmother Williams always served cornbread with this." Then, when your children marry or leave home, they will always know the favorite foods of each family member and how to make them.

Another good recipe to include comes from a friend of mine. It's her recipe for "Five-Minute Cookies" that children love. It's so simple—requires no baking—that the smallest child can make them. As a child's Christmas or birthday gift, my friend fills small baby-food or salad-dressing containers with the exact amount of each ingredient required for the cookies, and places them in a gift box together with the recipe written on the enclosed card. Girls and boys alike enjoy her fine gift and later boast they made the cookies all by themselves. Here is her recipe:

FIVE-MINUTE COOKIES
MAKES ABOUT 40 COOKIES

2 cups granulated sugar	3 cups uncooked oatmeal
4 tablespoons cocoa	½ cup peanut butter
1 cup milk	½ cup chopped nuts (any kind)
1 stick margarine	1 teaspoon vanilla extract

PASS IT ON

Combine sugar, cocoa, milk, and margarine in a saucepan. Let them come to a boil, stirring constantly. Boil for 1 minute, remove from heat, and add oatmeal, peanut butter, nuts, and vanilla extract.

Mix well and drop by teaspoonfuls on waxed paper to cool.

Every homemade cookbook should have this quick recipe. The cookies sell fast at bazaars, offer a fast dessert for unexpected guests and, as my friend suggests, the ingredients and recipe make a thoughtful and unusual gift for a child.

Perhaps, instead of a family cookbook, you would like to compile the recipes of famous people. Gathering their favorites will help you gather autographs at the same time. When writing celebrities for their favorite recipes, explain that you want them for your personal cookbook. It is wise to enclose a self-addressed stamped envelope. I find that most people reply when you do this.

Lyndon Johnson's recipe for chili made the rounds of Washington, D.C., cooks. Here it is, and you might start your own celebrity cookbook with it.

PEDERNALES RIVER CHILI
Serves 6

4 pounds coarsely ground round or chuck beef	6 teaspoons chili powder, or to taste
1 large onion, chopped	1½ cups canned whole tomatoes
2 cloves garlic	2 to 6 dashes hot-pepper sauce
1 teaspoon oregano	2 cups hot water
1 teaspoon cumin seed	Salt to taste

Place meat, onions and garlic in Dutch oven. Cook until lightly colored. Add oregano, cumin seed, chili powder, tomatoes, hot-pepper sauce, hot water, and salt to taste. Simmer 1 hour. Skim off fat and serve.

As a last piece of advice, I think your cookbook might benefit by including some of the traditional dining customs of your family and ancestors. For instance, in a well-ordered eighteenth-century Williamsburg dining room, the host and hostess always sat at opposite ends of the dining table, each ladling soup from a tureen, while the beautifully arranged "hot" main dishes stood cooling on the table. Carl Humelsine, President of Colonial Williamsburg Foundation, says "Our eighteenth-century forebears seldom expected hot food to be served hot—and be-

24

came accustomed to eating the finest culinary preparations lukewarm, and just as often, stone cold.''

Every nationality had its own customs, and most likely your parents continued some of these—passed down to them from their own parents. As America becomes more and more a melting pot, many of these traditions are being lost—as a nation, we've become Americanized. What better place to leave an account of how it used to be in your family than in your very own cookbook?

For instance, growing up during the depression, the only vacations we children enjoyed were perhaps a visit to a relative in our own state. But my ingenious mother saw to it that we had imaginary visits to all the countries of the world. Once a month we had a special "foreign" dinner, in which every member of the family participated.

We were told ahead of time what country we would visit, and each of us had to come up with some interesting fact about the country or its people. Mother always managed to get a recording or two of the country's music, which she played on our Victrola during the meal. The food was prepared in that nation's style, and I can still remember learning my first Spanish words at a Mexican dinner of chili and beans served at the family dining table.

These special foreign dinners were so popular that our friends often begged to be invited to them. My mother truly opened the window on the world for us, and in later years, when I was privileged to visit some of those countries, it really seemed that I had been there before. So I continued my mother's custom with my own children, and I suspect that my daughters will do the same with theirs.

It's this sort of thing, written down alongside your recipes, that will make your cookbook a family heirloom.

4

Trace Your Family Tree

MORE and more Americans are becoming "identity conscious." All of a sudden, everybody wants to know who they are, where they came from. Did you ever wonder if you had royal blood flowing through your veins? Or if you came from wealthy old aristocrats? On the other hand, did you ever wonder if you descended from horse thieves or bandits?

Whatever your reasons for searching your background, it is apparent that more and more of us want to know. Family pride seems to have had a rebirth.

There are mail-order houses getting rich off millions of Americans who will pay from $19.95 and up for "beautiful coats of arms"—unauthentic family crests. One mail-order house, Halbert's, Inc., feels that ancestral crests are here to stay. Halbert's is protected from "authenticity" guarantees by the disclaimer printed on every report: "This report does not represent individual lineage of (your name inserted here) family tree and no genealogical representation is intended or implied."

Despite this, millions continue to send away for unauthentic crests to call their own.

It is much more interesting and satisfying to trace your own lineage. It may take time, but tracing your ancestors can lead you down many interesting paths and often into strange and exotic lands. Unfortunately, many families did not keep records. (Do you?) That's probably why many young people these days seem to be scurrying to get the unwritten family histories from their elders who are still living.

Trace Your Family Tree

There are several ways to go about researching your family history and it is a thoughtful parent who records this history in writing and by having it documented or by establishing a family tree in paints or embroidery.

There are two things to remember. It's better to take one side of the family at a time (either paternal or maternal) and carry the research through several generations; and it's better to gather all the known information from relatives and available records before you begin to really search.

Prepare a questionnaire for every member of your family. Ask: Whom did cousin Charlie marry? Do you have any birth certificates of any family members, beyond your own family? Do you have a family Bible in which any records were kept? Such questions may turn up places and dates that you didn't dream were available and they will make your search so much easier.

After you have gathered all available data together, attempt to trace your family back to their arrival in this country. The Daughters of the American Revolution in Washington, D.C., have records going back to the Mayflower. Write to them, giving as many facts as you have.

For amateurs, it's better to start with your parents; from there, go to your grandparents, then to your great-grandparents. Work from the present to the past and go as far as you can with family documents or knowledge. Start this way:

Since most of us know our parents' date and place of birth, get their birth certificates by writing to the office of vital statistics in the county where they were born. In many states, a child's birth certificate carries such information as the place of birth of his or her parents, their full names and sometimes even their occupations.

If your grandparents' place of birth is in the United States, either the county, city, or state clerk's office will have birth records. In some areas, the department of health keeps the records, but the county or state will inform you where to go, if you write to them first. Try to obtain your grandparents' birth certificates for additional information about your great-grandparents.

For birth records outside of the United States, write to the office of vital statistics in the village or town in the country from which they came. If this is not known (some birth certificates simply say the parents came from France, Spain, or some other country, and do not give a city or town), you must try to ascertain what year they migrated to the United States and their port of entry.

27

PASS IT ON

The Morton Allan Directory of European Passenger Steamship arrivals is usually available in your public library. It gives the arrivals in New York from 1890 to 1930; Boston, Baltimore, and Philadelphia arrivals between 1904 and 1926. If this does not cover the time of your relative's arrival, you must go a step further.

More ships arrived in New York port than any other port but the records from 1874 to 1896 are not indexed, so it's important for you to know the name of the ship and date of arrival. This way you may find the port of departure, which will give you a key to tracing your relatives in their mother country.

If your ancestor became a citizen of this country, you may send $3 (1976 cost) to the Immigration and Naturalization Service, 119 D Street, NE, Washington, DC 20536 for an application (n-585). Give them the name and whatever details you have. Naturalization records hold much family background in their files.

You could also write to the Central Reference Division of the National Archives, Washington, DC 20408. They can look up passenger lists dating back to 1820, if you know the approximate time of arrival of your ancestor in America. They have a few records as far back as 1787. Again, it helps if you know the port of arrival.

If your relative arrived at a Pacific Coast port, many records were lost in the San Francisco fires in 1851 and 1920, but the California Historical Society, 2090 Jackson Street, San Francisco, California 94109 has many records of passenger arrivals from 1820 to 1869.

If you have determined the foreign country (and town) from which your ancestors migrated to the United States, write to the office of vital statistics in the capital of that county (and, if known) for birth and marriage data which will lead you to their parents.

If you trace back far enough, you will reach a point where surnames were acquired. Early history shows that first names were adequate until more than one John, Thomas, Richard, etcetera, occupied a village. Then it became necessary to add another name for identification. If one John was a baker, he became John Baker; if another was a farmer, he became John Farmer, and so on down the line. An interesting book, available in public libraries, is the Dictionary of American Family Names. It will give you much information about the origin of names, which may give you another clue to your family tree.

There are several ways to make your family tree so that it will become a treasured heirloom to your children. You may compile a family history in notebook form. This may include all the documents you have been able to gather. Of course, if you have more than one child, have photostats made of all materials, so that each child may have his own history book.

You may lightly draw the lines of an ordinary tree on the material to be embroidered. The trunk of the tree should represent the mother and father; the branches, each of the children; and the roots, the ancestors (see illustration). Make sure that when you embroider the tree, you

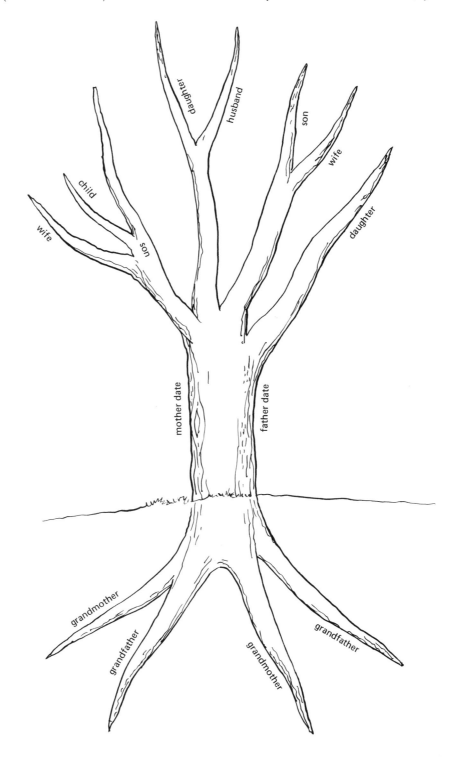

date	great grandmother		great grandmother	date
date	great grandfather		great grandfather	date
date	grandmother		grandmother	date
date	grandfather		grandfather	date
date	mother ———————		——————— father	date

child (date)   child (date)   child (date)

have the names and dates in the proper places. I like to leave extra branches for all the grandchildren who will come in the future.

Perhaps you would rather paint the tree, using the same procedure. Or perhaps you would prefer to draw a straight line near the bottom of a page with small lines pointing downward for each child; a straight line up the center of the page, with markers, starting at bottom, indicating parents; the next marker for grandparents and on up the scale as far as you want to go (see illustration).

There are more orthodox ways of making a "family tree," but I like the simple, original ones. After you've traced your ancestry, think of some way you would like to record the family history so that your children or their children will not have to go to all that trouble tracing it for themselves. They'll love you for it.

5

Unusual Easy-to-Make Quilts

WHEN the first women missionaries went to Hawaii back in 1820, they were shocked and alarmed to find that the women on the island wore no top garments, which left their breasts bare. Immediately, the missionaries set about teaching the natives to make loose nightgown-like garments (the first muumuus) and, being thrifty, they taught them to use the leftover scraps to make quilts. The native women began copying the beautiful foliage, flowers, and waterfalls in designs which they appliquéd on their quilts. Mealii Kalama is the most famous quiltmaker in Hawaii, having made over seven hundred quilts which have sold from $700 up. Many of the Hawaiian quilts are valuable heirlooms, the patterns having been passed down through families for generations. Some designs are so treasured that as soon as a quilt is finished, the design is destroyed and never revealed to anyone again.

Quilt-making was once a woman's work but times have changed. More and more men are taking up sewing crafts, and some of the loveliest handmade items displayed at craft shows are made by them. It's no longer considered "sissy" or unmasculine to thread a needle and create beautiful things by sewing.

My heirloom quilts are totally different from those intricate patterns our grandmothers used; nor do I take the months and months of constant work to complete a quilt that they spent. My Penny Puff Quilt is so simple a child can make it, yet it is beautiful; it can vary in design,

31

and it is as warm as any down-filled comforter you have. The nicest thing about making this quilt is that you can work on it anywhere, without quilting frames or cumbersome materials. It's made in tiny sections and then put together.

Penny Puff Quilt

The whole family can participate in this project, which makes the quilt more treasured by all. There is no expense involved, for the quilt is made from scraps and nylon hose that have outlived their usefulness. This is how it's done:

Accumulate all the discarded nylon hose you possibly can. Ask your friends to save them for you. If panty hose are used, cut them off at the top of the leg. Wash the hose in a net bag or pillowcase, using a sweet-smelling water softener.

Every piece of scrap material (you may use old clothing, too) should be cut into 6-inch squares. Try to have two of a kind (front and back) to be sewn together around three sides, inverted and filled with one rolled-up nylon stocking and a penny.

Close the opening and lay the filled square aside until you have enough squares to make the size quilt you want.

When you have enough filled squares, lay them out on a table or on the floor and form any design you like. You may have large blocks of varying colors or a large colorful block in the center, surrounded by lighter colors or white. There are many ways to assemble the squares.

When you have decided on your pattern, simply stitch the squares together edge to edge, either by hand or on the machine. Make sure that all are joined together on the reverse side of the quilt without overlapping.

This quilt is as puffy, soft, and warm as any other filled quilt, for the nylons, although light in weight, hold the warmth better than almost any other filling. The penny insertion is optional, but adds a great deal to the value of the quilt. Who knows, in a few years, the penny may become a thing of the past and these little coins hidden away in your quilt may become collector's items. In no way do they interfere with laundering.

Small-size quilts made of silk or satin squares make lovely baby quilts or carriage coverlets. If you decide to make one of these and want silks or satins for your squares, visit second-hand thrift shops and look for old satin slips or nightgowns which you can buy for very little. I have acquired the habit of cutting up old clothing or sewing scraps immediately

Penny puff quilt.

33

into 6-inch squares and putting them away in a box for future use. This saves space, and I'm ready to sew at the drop of a hat. On rainy days or days the youngsters can't go out to play, bring out the box and let them sew around the sides of the squares. You may have to do some of them over, but it will keep them busy and they will enjoy doing something worthwhile. If your children are pre-teen or in their teens and would like to have an unusual party, let them have a "quilting bee" and make a quilt. You'll be surprised at how much they will enjoy it and perhaps the quilt they make can be sold at a bazaar or benefit for their club or the scouts or some other worthy cause.

STORYBOOK QUILT

The storybook quilt is just as interesting to make and quite simple. Look through thrift shops for the cloth storybooks that are made for very young children. The pictures are on cloth pages and printed on one side only. Use these pages as border squares or centers for regular cotton patchwork quilts. A Winnie the Pooh quilt will delight any child. If you're fortunate enough to find several such books, you may make all your squares of them and use a plain sheet backing. I prefer using old blankets for lining because they're much easier to handle than cotton batting. Pictures should be sewn onto the quilt top and when the top is finished put all the layers together (top, lining, and back) and baste or secure with straight pins. Turn in the edges of the top and bottom pieces and stitch together, being careful to keep the lining smooth in-between. Remove basting or pins upon completion of quilting.

EMBROIDERED QUILT

I think it is the unusual quilt, the one that uses imagination and thoughtfulness, that makes the best heirloom. That's why I particularly like embroidered quilts.

Here is an extra-fine quilt which makes a beautiful wedding gift or a present for someone who is very special in your life.

Use linen, muslin, or regular cotton sheets for back and front. Solid colors are essential.

Iron on large embroidery transfer designs in center and around edges. If you have artistic ability, you may lightly sketch a design of flowers, basket, fruits, or whatever. One of the prettiest embroidered quilts I ever saw was done on linen with silk thread and was on sale in a shop for $1,500. There is no patchwork to be done on these quilts, so they are not too difficult. You'll need a large flat surface to work on and you must be very careful not to soil the sheets in handling them.

Embroider the top of the cover. The back should remain plain. Once you have finished the top, sandwich a wool or cotton blanket between the two sheets, then tack them with the same color thread as the sheets. Tack about every 1 inch, so that it holds securely. An embroidered edging is ideal for binding the quilt, although you may use bias binding of the same color.

This quilt may take longer to make than the others, but you'll have one of the most unusual and beautiful quilts ever seen anywhere, and one you'll be proud to pass on to your children as a family heirloom.

WASHING INSTRUCTIONS FOR FEATHERS

If you decide to use an old down-filled comforter as the filling for your quilt or coverlet top, wash the old comforter first. This applies to feather pillows you may wish to cover, too. These items are better washed by hand, following these instructions: Fill bath tub half full with lukewarm water and soft soap powder (never use detergent). Place your comforter or pillow in the tub and leave it overnight. Next morning, turn it and squeeze it gently to loosen all dirt. When the water is well soiled, remove the stopper (not the items) and refill the tub with clean water. Squeeze gently again and again, changing the water as often as soap suds appear in the water. Remove the stopper and allow the water to run out of the tub. Press down on the item, pushing as much water as possible out of it. Remove the item from the tub and place it in the washing machine, distributing it evenly. Run the machine on spin cycle only. Final drying should be done in a large dryer at low heat. When drying, add an old pair of tennis shoes to the dryer. The shoes will break up the wet clumps and the rubber in the shoes, bumping against the cover of the comforter or pillows will create a static electricity that will help fluff up the feathers.

SEWING TIPS

When piecing in a quilt, punch a small hole in the side of the same box you keep your quilt pieces in and put your spool of thread in the box too, leaving a small piece hanging out of the hole. This way, you never have to look for the thread or have it drop on the floor.

Embroidery floss becomes very tangled after you've unwound it. Cut a piece of cardboard, 5-by-1 inches, and insert into the skein of thread before using. This way the thread will unravel as you need it. Use a straight pin to hold the end of thread in place, when not in use.

We use straight pins in many of our crafts to hold materials in place. Various shades of nail polish are ideal for coloring the heads of pins, making them easier to find and remove. This is especially handy when instructing a child or craft beginner, because you may color the pin heads in the same color of thread to be used where pinned. This is useful in quilting.

A handy little "carry all" can be made from half a yard of material and an oatmeal box. When sewing a dress, try to manage to have half a yard of material left over. Trace the bottom of an oatmeal box onto cardboard. Increase the circle one inch. Measure both around the oatmeal box and lengthwise. Cut the material to size, adding half an inch on sides for seams and 2 inches at the top for a hem to hold the drawstring. This cover may be lined with material matching another dress so that it's reversible. Slip the oatmeal box inside and insert a drawstring of ribbon or tape. This little bag is pretty to carry with you or useful to hang on the hanger with your dress. You can store all the accessories that go with that particular dress, such as gloves, pins, etcetera in it.

Quilting has become so popular that quilters are forming organizations to exchange tips, share their craft, and put on quilt shows where their quilts sell for high prices. A Northern Virginia organization, Quilters Unlimited, in a few short years has grown into five chapters with over two hundred members. A young housewife and former school teacher in Maryland, who learned quilting from her grandmother, gets as much as $900 per quilt for those she is commissioned to do. If you have time and patience, quilting is truly a profitable hobby to have.

Although quilting dates back to the twelfth century and perhaps beyond, patchwork quilts are strictly an American "invention." American colonists found winters cold and rugged and very rough on the quilts that they had brought with them from their homelands. Before flax could be grown and sheep raised and sheered to furnish looms and spinning wheels with materials for making fabrics, their original quilts had become worn and torn. Since there were no new materials with which to make new quilts, it became necessary to patch the old ones.

Before the days of photograph albums and statisticians, the American quilt kept the family records. From materials used in a quilt, one could judge, many years later, if the quilt had been made in good times or bad. In bad times, quilts were made of bits and pieces of clothing from every member of the family, including father's Revolutionary uniform.

Often the pieces were identified with stitches. You could easily tell from the condition of the scraps how long the garments had been worn before being discarded. The smaller the patchwork, the harder the times; for it indicated that even scraps of material were hard to come by. These "hard times" quilts encompassed varied materials, mixed together in one quilt: silks, woolens, and cottons rested side by side in a single cover.

When times were good and a family prosperous, a quilt could contain squares of fine imported materials from Italy, England, or France. The colors were bright, not faded and thin from years of rough wear as were the pieces taken from garments used to keep the body warm. The squares were often larger and a quilt would be of one kind of material: cotton, silk, or wool. Many early records of our country refer to quilts. They were mentioned in wills and record books, often telling what ship the material came over on and how much it cost. There are records of estate sales that mention quilts. From the Fairfax Estate in Belvoir, Virginia, there is an account of George Washington buying nineteen "coverlids" (quilts) to take home to Martha in Mount Vernon.

Bicentennial quilts are now all the rage. Bells, historical figures, log cabins, maps, Indians, and other appliqués are becoming popular all over again. No matter what kind of quilt you decide to make, embroider your name and date somewhere on the quilt. If it is plainly marked, it will be much more valuable in years to come.

6

Coverlets

COVERLETS are popular as wall hangings, bedspreads, and throws for upholstered furniture. One of the easiest to make is the "pouf" coverlet.

POUF COVERLET

Make a cardboard circle about 4 inches in diameter or smaller. Most antique coverlets are of a smaller pouf, but it's easier to work with the 4-inch size. At 4 inches the pouf will be a good size when drawn, and the work will go faster; however, a smaller one makes a more delicate pouf.

Save scraps from sewing and old clothes. Any fabric will do, as long as it's not too thick, not too thin, and doesn't ravel easily. Woolens are generally too thick, silks too thin (although two circles of sheer silk can be sewn together and used as one piece).

Using your cardboard pattern, cut circles out of the fabric. You can pile fabric on top of fabric and cut several circles at one time.

To make the pouf, thread your needle with a double length of thread. (You'll want the thread to be strong so it won't break later when the pouf is being handled.) Hide the knot inside the hem of the circle. (See step 1 in illustration.) Hem all around the circle. The size of stitches doesn't matter but a large stitch goes faster and gathers easily. When the hem has been completed, pull the thread as tightly as possible, gathering the pouf. Tie the thread securely.

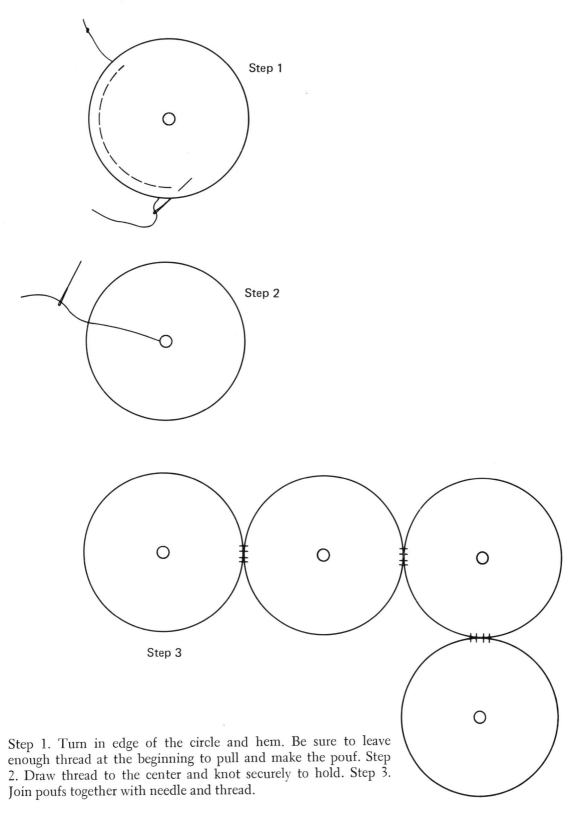

Step 1

Step 2

Step 3

Step 1. Turn in edge of the circle and hem. Be sure to leave enough thread at the beginning to pull and make the pouf. Step 2. Draw thread to the center and knot securely to hold. Step 3. Join poufs together with needle and thread.

39

PASS IT ON

Sew the poufs together just enough to connect them. Make sure they are going to come out in straight lines. If you sew them at different points, they won't come out in a straight line. Lay them out on something flat and make sure they will be connected evenly (see step 3 in illustration).

Sewn together, poufs make pretty, lacy-looking coverlets. They definitely have an heirloom look. This circle work is very popular in England

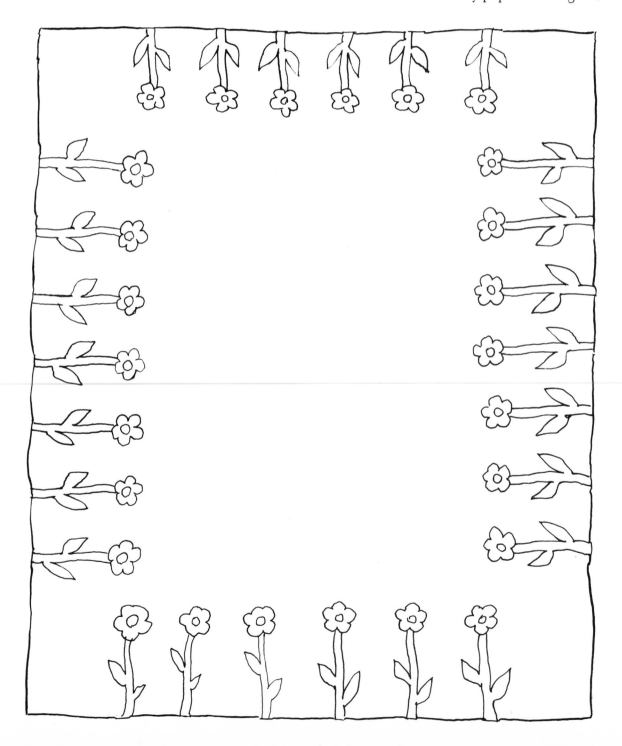

now, as it was with our ancestors in colonial days. Understandably, the antique pouf work you find in shops was often done with very tiny poufs, for our thrifty forebears used every precious scrap of material. It has other advantages, too. A pouf coverlet is a sort of quilt, for the poufs, after drawing, are double material and give the warmth of a quilt, without the filling of one.

Poufs sewn on solid backing, such as sheets, make attractive coverlets. You may arrange the poufs as flowers, use bias binding as stems, and appliqué them onto the solid-color backing. Or you can arrange them all around the backing as shown in illustration.

HAPPY-FACE COVERLET

The idea of making this Happy-Face Coverlet came to me after watching some children at the zoo carrying balloons on which a "happy face" had been stamped. The first one I made was so popular with my children that it accompanied them to rock festivals and "sleep-ins" until it became threadbare. I guarantee that every young person will treasure one and that if you have more than one youngster in your home, you'd better make one for each of them, if you want to avoid a family fight over who gets to use the one you have.

My first Happy-Face Coverlet was made on a simple cotton blanket that had seen better days. I debated over using the blanket as a lining for a quilt, but decided to simply appliqué "happy faces" all over it and let the girls use it for their outings. Happy faces may be applied to sheets, blankets, or old, solid-color bedspreads that are unattractive. Seven yards of muslin will make a beautiful coverlet for a bed, if you would rather work with new materials.

Cut a cardboard circle of the desired size for the faces you want. I use a 9-inch plate or pie tin. For a double blanket or sheet, it takes twenty happy faces of this size; arranged four across in five rows top-to-bottom.

Use yellow or orange material for the faces. The material must be a solid color for the best effect. Cut all your circles at once. Stack them, one on top of the other, with regular carbon paper between each one. On the top circle, draw your "happy face" as shown in illustration. (You can, of course, change the expression by changing the curve of the mouth, and doing the eyes differently.)

Remove the carbon paper and you're ready to embroider with a regular outline stitch. Embroider each circle before appliquéing it to the cover. Petals of the same material appliquéd around the face will give a sunflower effect, which is most attractive.

41

Buttonhole
stitch

Coverlets

Pin your faces on the cover, spacing them properly. Use the button-hole stitch to appliqué them on.

MEMORY COVERLETS

The year our twin girls were eight we moved to North Carolina. As I started packing, I realized it would be foolish to take along all their out-grown clothes, but there was a pair of matching dresses from their toddler age that I simply couldn't part with. Surely there was some way I could preserve them, without packing them back in a drawer.

Then the idea hit me. Why not appliqué a dress to the middle of a plain bedspread. My mother had embroidered a spread many years before. She used a Dutch-girl pattern that showed a dress and bonnet, without a face. It had been one of my favorites. I had two Bates spreads of heavy white cotton that the girls used on their bunk beds, so I folded the dresses and put them away with the spreads for a future time, after we had become settled in our new home.

Select your backing; use a plain, solid-color bedspread, sheet, muslin fabric, or blanket.

Appliquéd, quilted coverlet for crib. *Courtesy Appalachian Spring*

Coverlets

Select the pieces of clothing you want to use on the Memory Coverlet. For girls, use a simple dress (no ruffles or frills) that can be pressed flat and applied by appliquéing to the middle of the cover. Pin it in place or baste it before finally stitching. The dress may be stitched by machine or by hand. If hand sewing is done, use the buttonhole stitch with thread that is the same color as the dress. Sew around the entire dress: skirt, bodice, arms, and neck. Make sure there are no parts (such as pockets) free from stitching. You may use a tacking or a quilting stitch all over the dress, if desired. Remember the coverlet will be washed many times, and there should be no part of the dress that is not fastened down; otherwise it may come apart in washing machine.

After the dress is completely sewn down, with a pencil, lightly write the child's name and the year the dress was worn below the dress. With colored embroidery thread, embroider over the outline so that the notation becomes permanent. I suggest that you use the full six strands of embroidery floss, because frequent washings have a tendency to break the threads when they are left thin (see illustration).

Stand back and look at your cover. If you feel it needs a little more decoration, try four colorful socks appliquéd to the corners.

Small boys' outfits are done much the same way. There are a few things to remember. If the fly of the child's pants has a zipper, remove it and stitch the fly closed. If the belt has a metal buckle, remove it. Buttons do not interfere with washing, although they should be sewn on as tightly as possible. If you think it adds to your cover, you may want to outline the collar with black embroidery floss or, perhaps, touch up the outfit in places with special stitches of your own. A lot depends on how colorful the outfits are. If there is braid or rick-rack on the garments, make sure it is stitched to the cover in all places. This reinforces the original thread, so that the braid will not come loose in laundering.

FAMILY COVERLET

This is a personalized coverlet that also makes an unusual quilt top. It will become a true heirloom that is treasured by every member of your family.

Buy 6 yards of 36-inch muslin. Cut it into 3-yard pieces. Stitch the material lengthwise, making a cover 72 by 108 inches. (A sheet may be used.)

Have each member of the family trace his and her hands (opened wide) onto cardboard. This makes your pattern for patches that will be applied to the coverlet.

45

PASS IT ON

Cut out each member's hands from clothing belonging to that person. Dad's shirts make nice patches, so do cotton shorts or pants. If you have small children, the patches will vary in sizes and may be scattered all over the cover in any design you like.

Appliqué the hand designs onto the material, use buttonhole stitches. Beneath each hand, embroider the name of the person whose hand it is.

In the corner of the coverlet, embroider the family name and date.

I attended a friend's family reunion a few years ago and each member of the family from the great-grandmother to the smallest great-grandchild had their hands traced onto poster paper and marked for identification. The following year, she told me, there was a family coverlet hanging on the wall of the dining room when she visited her parents. Her grandmother had finished the piece in one year, although she was in her late eighties.

This could be a fun project for the whole family and new "hands" can be added as the family increases.

7

Samplers

ALMOST every family of the past had one or more samplers hanging somewhere in their homes. The most popular one was "God Bless Our Home," which often hung just inside the front door for everyone to see. These old samplers from the past are much sought after in antiques shops and are treasured by those who were fortunate enough to have them passed down to them. Many of them were dated and well-preserved under glass. I have seen one dated 1812 that was in mint condition; it was a very valuable piece of Americana, for it had to do with the war of that year.

Conventional samplers make nice heirlooms, but not nearly as nice as the personal ones you can do for your own family. Wedding and birth samplers are becoming increasingly popular and are unusually pretty when you combine two or more of the crafts mentioned in this book. Here are directions for making them:

PRESSED FLOWERS AND EMBROIDERY SAMPLER

A ready-made linen tea towel, a piece of linen cut from the bottom of a skirt, or a piece of unbleached muslin, in the size you wish to frame, is ideal as background for your sampler.

Center a piece of carbon paper where the embroidery will go; then place a piece of lined tablet or notebook paper over it. In your best

47

longhand, write the name, birthdate, and weight of your child when he or she was born. For example:

Sally Ann Brunner
Born
April 24, 1953
Weight
5 pounds, 11 ounces

Embroider in 3-ply embroidery cotton (color of your choice) over the writing which should have been traced clearly on your cloth.

After the embroidery is done, lay your sampler on heavy cardboard and begin decorating the sides with your pressed flowers and grasses. Use a white glue (Elmer's is fine), putting it on with a toothpick, which will slide under your arrangement. When the decorations are in place, put your glass on top, and using the cardboard as a backing, fit your frame around it.

The same procedure may be used for a wedding sampler which might read:

Sandra M. Brunner
Wedded to
Charles Pfefferle
March 3, 1973

A decoupage sampler may include baby pictures around the birth announcement, or pictures of the bride and groom around the wedding sampler. There is no limit to the ways samplers can be made into beautiful, very personal treasures for those for whom they are made. A wedding sampler makes an ideal wedding or anniversary gift for your son, daughter, or a friend.

If you want your sampler to be especially beautiful, do it on satin or velvet; however, satin will not hold up as well as linen and muslin. A friend of mine made a wedding sampler for her daughter on a satin coverlet she had used as a baby. I like to date all my needlecrafts but it's not necessary. By putting your initials and the date in a tiny corner, there will be no question, years from now, as to who made it or when it was made. This is sometimes important when they are passed down to grandchildren and great-grandchildren.

Samplers may be embroidered all over, hand-painted, or decorated in many ways. They can be about many things: a favorite poem, your first real home, or a graduation that meant a lot to your family. Most of the old ones you find in antiques shops were of a religious nature. A very dear old lady I once knew had a great deal of faith in Saint Anthony, and she made samplers for all her nine children that read: "Dear Saint Anthony, come around; something's lost and can't be found." She believed that such a prayer would restore anything a person had lost. I was so impressed with her samplers that I never forgot the message she had embroidered on them.

Some of the antique samplers that you see are morbid. I feel strongly that a sampler should be a happy reminder, filled with inspiration and cheerfulness. A happy thought spreads sunshine, and what better heirloom can we pass down to our children than a ray of sunshine that will stir happy memories long after we are gone?

Embroider a little happiness; weave a happy thought into your embroidery, and paint it with beauty that will uplift all who see it. This will be the heirloom that money can't buy, the heirloom that will build a bridge between our generation and those who come after.

8

Braiding

HISTORICALLY, Americans come from rugged stock. While the men were out hewing logs for houses in the wilderness of the new world, the women were busy with the handcrafts that made their houses into cozy and comfortable homes. Whether quilting or braiding, they were seldom without a needle and thread. In those early days, it took three to four months to make a braided rug. After strips were cut from old clothing, they were folded by hand, pressed, then sewn and rolled into balls to await the time when there was sufficient material to make a rug. The whole family participated in the rug-making, and neighbors did, too.

Today, with the handy little metal gadgets called folders, and the long, flat needle-like tools called lacers, the task is so easy and simple that a child can make a rug. Braiding time on a room-size rug has been shortened from months to days. No longer are braided rugs sewn with one side rough and ugly, the tied threads and the back of stitches showing. By lacing, a rug is reversible and both sides are equally pretty.

Craft shops sell the folders (you need three) and the lacers, but you may prefer to buy a kit that is complete with all the tools and instructions you need. They are inexpensive (about $3) and can be used over and over again.

Braiding

Materials

Woolen or cotton material to be cut into strips and braided
Cardboard 1½ inches wide, 1 foot long for use as cutting guide
3 folders
Needle and thread
Heavy string

Directions

Cut a piece of cardboard 1½ inches wide and about a foot long. Use this as a guide for cutting your strips of material. Lay the cardboard on the edge of your material and cut alongside. This way all your strips will be 1½ inches wide.

Insert a strip of material through each of the three folders. Slide it through the bar opening and the strips will come out of the small end, folded and ready for braiding. If you do not have folders, do it the old-fashioned way by folding the strips, both sides to the middle, and then folding the entire strip, so that the rough edges are inside the fold. You will need to press the folded strip and baste it to keep the folds intact.

At one end, sew the three strips together, using a buttonhole stitch so that the end is tightly secured and no rough edges show.

Either place a heavy object on the end of the strips or if you have a heavy board, tack the ends of the strips to the board so you can braid tautly without the material moving. This way, your braids will be tight and evenly done.

It's easier to work with short pieces of material, so I always sew my additional strips on as I go. To add strips, cut ends on the bias, sew the old and new ends together, and trim off the edges close to stitches.

The overall size of your rug will depend on the size of your center circle. Use this chart to determine the size of the rug you will make:

2-by-3-foot oval rug   = 12-inch center circle
3-by-4 foot oval rug   = 12-inch center circle
3-by-5-foot oval rug   = 2-foot center circle
4-by-6-foot oval rug   = 2-foot center circle
5-by-7-foot oval rug   = 2-foot center circle
6-by-9-foot oval rug   = 3-foot center circle
8-by-10-foot oval rug = 3-foot center circle
9-by-12-foot oval rug = 3-foot center circle

With good, heavy carpet string (or wrapping twine) start lacing the center circle from the fold back to the original sewn end. If you are

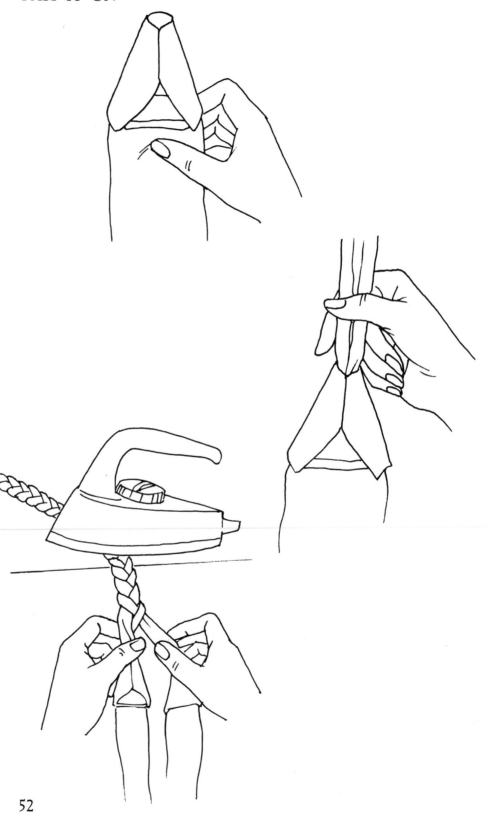

52

fortunate enough to have a heavy board, such as mentioned above, and a thin nail (which you used to tack down the first braiding) you may lace toward the nail, lift the center off the nail, and reverse the ends, hooking it back over the nail. The rug is much easier to handle this way. Continue braiding more strips and lacing them to the center. When the thread begins to run out, simply tie on additional thread without unlacing your needle; there will be no difficulty pushing the thread through the braids.

When the rug gets too big for lap or table work, you'll need to work on the floor. A friend of mine made all her rugs on the floor, adding a circle a night. The rug actually grew to room size right on the floor, as it was being walked on.

Your rug design is up to you. You may dye your materials and have a solid-color rug or mix and match colors so that you have a border of one color and a center of another color. Woolen materials are best for room-size rugs. I find old woolen army blankets or other woolen blankets the easiest materials to work with, although you can use men's pants, winter coats, and almost any other woolen garments. It's important to keep your strips of material about the same thickness. You will have difficulty if one strip is heavier than another.

If you do not buy the rug kit with folders, your material must be folded and basted to conceal the ragged edges. Folders eliminate hand basting as they fold the rough edges inside each strip.

A handmade braided rug is very expensive to buy. A woman I know charges $300 to make one for you and you furnish all the materials. So it's easy to see that a braided rug can become an heirloom your children will cherish, and the life of such a rug, under normal wear and tear, can extend to fifty or a hundred years.

A cotton braided rug is pretty, but it's not as durable as a woolen one. If you do not have enough woolen material to make a rug, visit thrift shops (summertime is better) and buy old blankets. Woolens are cheaper in summer, and there is less demand for blankets then. Even if a blanket is "holey," buy it. You can get a lot of good strips from it. Blankets are especially good for braiding, because they give you more material of one color to work with and you can plan your design with more ease.

Make sure your material is clean. Wash it with detergent, for this will discourage moths and kill any moth eggs that might be in the material. If a rug is worth doing, it's worth time and trouble and planning, for your finished rug will be a valuable treasure for many years to come.

53

9

Pressed Flowers

THE beauty and charm of our spring and summer flower gardens need not die when the snows come. Pressing flowers at their peak is one of the most popular ways of preserving them, and pressed-flower pictures have long been a popular form of art. During the Victorian era, many ladies found pressing and framing their arrangements a most delightful and "ladylike" pastime. Many of these Victorian flower pictures found their way into art galleries and museums and can be seen today.

Several years ago, while doing research to restore her big Victorian farmhouse in Washington, D.C., Sunny O'Neil became fascinated with the almost-forgotten art of pressed-flower pictures. She loved working with flowers, and at one time had made dried-flower arrangements for our Embassy in Brussels at the request of Mrs. John Eisenhower, whose husband was then Ambassador.

At home in Washington, Sunny set up a studio next to her farmhouse kitchen. It was large enough to display her pictures, and she could work with her glue and flowers on a big round table and still keep an eye on her kitchen and family. Her specialty was mixed bouquets that seem to bloom against the traditional black velvet, beautifully placed in antique gold and silver frames. Some of her arrangements were as much as three feet square, but she also placed dainty little nosegays with miniature ferns, rosebuds, small flowers, and pretty grasses to form what she calls her "Williamsburg Arrangement."

54

A silver-framed arrangement by Sunny O'Neil. *Photo by Terry Arthur*

55

A nosegay by Sunny O'Neil. *Photo by Terry Arthur*

56

Pressed Flowers

So many Washington notables wanted them that her hobby has become full-time work, and she was invited to teach classes in pressed-flower pictures at the Smithsonian Institution. Sunny O'Neil tells us that making pressed-flower pictures is easy. "Anyone can do it," she says. "All you need is a little time, a few flowers, and some glue."

Here are some sample flower-pressing tips, many of them culled from her own booklet, *Pressing Flowers for Lasting Beauty*.

HOW TO COLLECT YOUR FLOWERS

Grow some, buy some, find some; when you walk the dog and see a perfect posy in your neighbor's yard, ring the doorbell and ask if you may have it. If you're out driving, look for pretty flowers that grow wild in the meadows and along the roadside. Of course, when someone gives you a bouquet, sneak out one or two for your collection while they're still fresh.

Some blossoms are too fragile to press, and a few kinds lose all their color and look nondescript. Some color change can always be expected, but most flowers will look beautiful, anyway. Lily-of-the-valley, for instance, turns yellow, but is still valued for its delicate lines. Many blossoms are too bulky to press as a whole—but we'll show you how to work with those, too.

Among good flowers for pressing are: acacia, ageratum, anemone, aster, baby's-breath, buttercups, black-eyed susan, blue lace flower, clematis, columbine, coral bells, cornflower, dogwood, forget-me-nots, forsythia, geranium, larkspur, marigolds, narcissus, pansy, poppy, primrose, rose, Queen Anne's lace, spirea, statice, sweet alyssum, verbena, yarrow, and zinnias—and don't forget ferns, leaves, and grasses.

If you're gathering flowers from your own garden, carry around a box, basket, or even a kitchen colander to place them in. Don't pick too many at a time—no more than thirty or so—take them in and press them at once.

If you're out looking for wild flowers, take along one or two "traveling" flower presses to keep them fresh till you get them home. Here's a simple one Sunny O'Neil suggests you make.

MAKE A "TRAVELING" FLOWER PRESS

For each press, you will need to cut 2 oblongs of heavy cardboard from packing boxes that are 10-by-12 inches each. Cut 2 pieces of binding tape, each 1 yard long. You'll also need 2 blotters and 2 sheets of absorbent paper that is cut to fit.

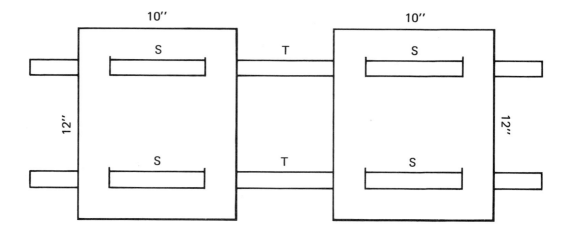

On both of the cardboards, cut 2 slits (S), top and bottom on either side. (See the diagram.) Then thread 1 piece of binding tape (T) through the top slits of both cardboards. Thread the second tape through the bottom slits, and that's all there is to it.

When you pick flowers in your travels, place them on a blotter on one side of the press. Place the other blotter carefully over them and fold the top over. Tie the ends of the tape to hold the press securely closed. Your flowers will travel well. Transfer them to your permanent press as soon as you get them home.

PRESSING YOUR FLOWERS

Pressing Equipment

Old telephone books or other thick, heavy books, such as old wallpaper sample books, make good presses. Besides these, you'll need plain white blotting paper, cut to page size, and some bricks or other heavy objects to weigh them down.

To Press Your Flowers

It's best to press each flower and bud separately. Work with one species at a time. Remove all stems and discard most of them. Place the flowers carefully on a piece of blotting paper, flattening the centers and spreading the petals evenly. Don't overcrowd; space them so they don't touch each other. When one page is filled up, cover it carefully with another sheet of blotting paper. Then, place this blotting-paper sandwich between the pages of your pressing book, as near to the spine as possible. Close the book carefully and press it down with bricks, heavy books, or some other weight.

Press flower stems, leaves, and grasses in the same way, but remember to press stems, grasses, and flower stalks in natural curves—never stiff and straight.

58

Pressed Flowers

Always leave at least an inch of unused book between pressings.

Set the book, undisturbed, for at least five or six weeks in a well-ventilated place that's not too warm. (If flowers dry out too quickly, they become brittle and hard to handle.) Use them any time after that.

To Store

You can store your flowers in the pressing book or, if you need the space, store them flat between blotters in a well-sealed polyethylene bag.

ARRANGING YOUR PRESSED FLOWERS

Materials

By the time your flowers are ready, you should have searched attics and antiques shops for interesting old frames. The frame often dictates the style and design you will use. Have on hand a supply of felt and velvet for backgrounds. You'll also need long-handled tweezers to lift the delicate petals and white resin glue, such as 3M wood and paper glue, to fix your arrangements in place. Finally, you'll need to spray a lacquer or clear satin finish over all.

Method

Make your background: Cut a piece of cardboard slightly smaller than the back opening of the frame, and cover it with felt or velvet. Fold the edges to the wrong side and glue them down with your white resin glue. (Hold them in place with Scotch tape until they're dry.) If your frame has a mat, cover it in the same way.

With a tweezer, gently pick up your flowers, stems, leaves, grasses, etcetera, and place them on the background. Move them around until the arrangement pleases you. The arrangement can be quite simple, as in this "Pressed Wild Rose" of Sunny O'Neil's, in which the curved stems dictate the overall design.

To glue them down: Put some white resin glue onto a piece of aluminum foil, and use a toothpick or tiny "paddle" as an applicator. One by one, lift the flowers and other elements with your tweezer, take a tiny dab of glue on your toothpick and slide it underneath the flower or leaf at its central point. After gluing the center of a flower, slide a dab of glue under each of the petals.

For stems and grasses place a few tiny dabs of glue at the ends and a few strategic points underneath, to hold the curved shape.

When your arrangement is all glued down, place a piece of waxed paper on top to protect it; gently press down with your fingertips at all

59

A pressed wild rose by Sunny O'Neil. *Photo by Terry Arthur*

60

Pressed Flowers

glued points. Let dry thoroughly. When dry, check for any corners or spots that did not adhere. Reglue these, and let dry, again.

When everything is properly dry, lightly spray all over with a lacquer or other clear satin finish. Dry, then lightly spray again. Repeat four or five times, and your arrangement will be permanent.

OTHER TIPS AND FLORAL FANCIES

- Very thin, fragile petals may be glued to colored tissue paper (or toilet paper) giving the petal reinforcement and also adding color (which will show through the thin petals).
- For flowers that fade as they dry, paint watercolor on the petals—provided that they're "waterproof" and don't shrivel when wet. Dip a watercolor brush first in straight liquid detergent (or diluted powder) and then in your watercolor. Then lightly touch the brush to the petal and the color will transfer at once. With this method, you can turn pale pinks into deep pinks, and the effect is beautiful.
- If you have a flower with a very thick center, gently take off the petals and then trim down the back of the flower center with a razor blade. When the center is thin enough, glue it down, re-assemble and glue down the petals around it.
- Real mounted butterflies (or cutouts from magazines) may be added to your arrangements for beauty and effect.
- If you have a framed floral print that isn't particularly pretty or colorful, remove it from its frame and glue some of your pressed flowers to the print, matching flowers where possible, or even adding some. After gluing them, spray with lacquer as usual. This will change an ordinary picture into one of lasting beauty.
- Pressed flowers may also be used for decorating invitations, place cards, and other correspondence to add a special personal touch. Don't forget to spray lightly with lacquer, although once will be enough for these.
- Pressed-flower arrangements look especially pretty under glass on coffee tables or on serving trays.
- Tall grasses (with their seed pods at top) or long-stemmed flowers may be glued to plain lampshades, wastebaskets, and other household items. After gluing, spray with lacquer as for regular framed arrangements.

A last word: When your pressed-flower arrangement is framed and ready to hang, be sure to place it where it will not receive too much light: Even after they have been sprayed with lacquer, bright sunlight will fade the flowers.

61

10

The Art of Drying Flowers

LATE summer and early fall are the best times to gather flower and plant materials for drying. If you want to enhance that plain vase or flower pot, collect attractive plants from wherever you can—yards, fields, and forests. If you haven't dried flowers for a few years, you're in for a pleasant surprise. Arrangements are no longer dull, brownish, or monotonous. A few years back, the only plants selected for drying were those that dried in tones of brown, but with modern methods of drying, vivid colorful flowers, green grasses, leaves, and seed pods can be beautifully preserved.

Mississippi State University floriculturist, Ralph Null, advises you to gather the most perfect flowers for drying. Gather twice as many as you think you'll need, for some will be lost in the drying process. Noon is the best time of day to gather your plants, since that's the time when most of them are at their peak of dryness.

The methods for drying are fairly easy and the results are pleasing. One way to dry flowers and grasses is to hang them by the stems in a dark room. This process is called "air drying." Cut the flowers before they are fully opened (mature ones may fall apart during the drying process), then remove the foliage and gather the flowers loosely in small bunches which you can keep together with a rubber band. Hang them upside down in a well-ventilated place that is dark, dry, and warm. The following flowers are best for air drying: Bells of Ireland, strawflowers,

62

baby's-breath, everlasting flowers, Chinese lanterns, cockscomb, curled dock, goldenrod, mullein, astilbe, globe amaranth, and yarrow.

Generally, flowers that do not wilt easily can be air dried while those that wilt should be dried by one of the following methods:

2 parts borax to 1 part dry white sand

The amount used depends on the number of plants being dried. Use plants that are as free from surface moisture as possible. You may leave the stems or remove them below the base of the calyx. (Floral stem wires may be substituted for natural stem in final arrangements.) Prepare a box (a shoe box will do) by sprinkling the mixture of borax and sand over the bottom of the box. Place flowers or plants in the box and sprinkle them generously with remaining mixture (only one layer to a box, with flowers barely touching). Make sure you cover the entire plant. Be very careful not to crush or tear the petals. When plants are completely covered, there should be no air space around them. Seal the box and store at room temperature for a week or ten days.

Flowers that have been in water with a solution of flower preservative (such as florists use) may not dry properly with this method. Many people fail to dry florist flowers because of the preservative solution used. Dried flowers whose stems have been removed should be dried a second time if the petals are to be painted with watercolors (use the same process as before). Lay down each flower separately with space between them, so that the petals do not touch. For coloring the petals, saturate the brush in straight liquid detergent before dipping it in a watercolor so that the color will transfer to the petal.

Borax removes moisture from the blossoms and leaves and prevents wilting. Flowers that dry well by the borax method include: candytuft, coleus leaves, daisy, gloxinia, lilac, lily, lily-of-the-valley, marigolds, narcissus, Queen Anne's lace, pansy, roses, snapdragons, sunflowers, violets, zinnias, anemone, asters, calendulas, chrysanthemum, clematis, columbine, cosmos, dahlias, delphiniums, dianthus, dicentra, fuchsia, larkspur, tulips, buddleia, iberis, lupines, poppies, rudbeckia, scabiosa, spirea, and gladiolas.

1 part borax to 2 parts corn meal

Use the same method as for borax and sand.

There is a commercial preparation that does about the same as the borax mixtures. It is silica gel, which may be purchased from plant stores. It has directions for use in the package, but I have found the

63

formula for the borax-sand and borax–corn-meal just as effective; just substitute the gel for the borax.

1 part glycerine with 2 parts water

This method is primarily used for preserving foliage. The best results are obtained when foliage is treated in late summer, because foliage absorbs more of the solution at that time.

Either crush or split the stems and place in about 5 inches of glycerine solution. Leave foliage in solution until the leaves change color all the way to their edges. This may take ten days to two weeks. Wipe leaves often with a cloth moistened with glycerine solution.

Some leaves change color. Others do not. Green leaves may turn brown. The color they turn depends largely on the type of plant, the time of year, and the length of time they are left in the solution. Most foliage becomes satiny smooth after this process and can be used in a fresh flower arrangement without damage to it.

Dried-flower arrangements combined with driftwood, small logs, or some other outdoor base make lovely gifts and can be made so permanent in their beauty and durability that they can be considered part of your heirlooms. Various sprays, including regular hair spray, spray starch, and spray lacquer or sealer will add years to the preservation of your arrangement. Then too, your arrangement may be put into a shadow-box frame (see chapter 21) and covered with glass by cutting a basket in half and gluing it to the back of the frame as a container for your arrangement. An oatmeal box, with the top removed and cut in half lengthwise will serve the same purpose. (Anything that makes a cup to hold flowers will do.) These boxes may be painted any color and will look very professional when finished. Such a shadow-box arrangement of dried mosses, highlighted with scallop, helix, and cockle shells, circa 1865, hangs in the Sheldon Museum, in Middlebury, Vermont, which proves that the life of dried arrangements can be extended to a hundred years or more.

Experiment with your arrangements. Dried arrangements might serve well for wedding flowers or special occasions. What son or daughter would not be proud to say, "My mother [or father] made these"?

11

Decoupage

ALTHOUGH the art of decoupage may have originated as far back as three thousand years ago when the inhabitants of Siberia were cutting out decorations from felt and gluing them on things such as earthen jugs and water containers made of leather or skin, the decoupage process as a popular art form came to light during the eighteenth century, when European craftsmen produced imitations of painted Japanese and Chinese lacquered wares. Felt, an unwoven material made from wool, hair, and fur, and matted together by moisture, heat, rolling, beating, and pressure, was used in Asia during ancient times for tents, hats, coats, carpets, and for decorative purposes. Only the extremely wealthy could afford the original lacquered items that were imported from the Orient and the new art of "decoupage" became a popular substitute; so popular, in fact, that the ladies of the French court, including Marie Antoinette, took it up as an elegant pastime.

In Italy, the process became known as *"l'arte del povero"* or poor man's art. In France, they called it *"l'art scriban,"* a term they still use today. Marie Antoinette used the term *"decoupure"* to describe a lacy, valentine-like ornament she had cut out herself around 1780. About the same time a book appeared on the London market called, *Ladies Amusement, or The Whole Art of Japanning Made Easy.* It contained 1,500 hand-colored pictures of flowers, birds, shells, and other popular designs suitable for cutting and pasting to decorate "anything from a superb cabinet to the smallest toilet article."

65

PASS IT ON

Many enthusiasts collected pictures from all over the world for their art. One eighteenth-century Italian writer wrote: "Women are mad enough to cut engravings worth one hundred lire apiece. If this fashion continues, they will cut up Raphaels!"

"Do-it-yourself" art is flourishing in America today. Americans are glorifying the handmade, homemade objects as never before in our history. Decoupage kits are being sold in hobby shops by the millions, but original decoupage designs that you make yourself are much more fun. These are the ones you and your family will treasure more than the custom-made ones.

Decoupage is a delicate and colorful method of pasting on beautiful pictures, which are smooth and evenly put together, to form a composite picture. At first glance, it seems to be hand-painted. Well-done decoupage is an art form in itself. It may be done on paper, wood, glass, or metal; each piece is unique in design and effect. You form your own original picture by combining cutouts of many other pictures.

It is an art which will work on just about any surface but plastic. The beginner should select small boxes, jars, or perhaps wastebaskets to experiment on. It's essential to collect many pictures, all neatly cut out, before starting. To become proficient, one needs a sense of color, an eye for design and very clever, nimble fingers, along with lots of patience. This has never been an afternoon's work; rather it requires days and days of tedious cutting, arranging, and pasting and, perhaps, as many as thirty or forty coats of finish, while sanding, repeatedly, between finishes.

A friend of mine makes beautiful ladies' purses with wooden boxes. He applies old Christmas card cherubs, pictures of Hummel figures, photographs, or just about any picture you may want on them. Similar purses sell in specialty shops anywhere from $65 to $100. Artistic articles, such as these, will become real heirlooms; they will be as beautiful a hundred years from now as they were when first made.

Many decoupage pictures hang in museums all over the world. There are also vases which look much like hand-painted pieces but are really decoupage over pottery.

DECOUPAGING PICTURES

Weeks before you get down to the actual decoupaging, start collecting cutouts—flowers, children, birds, animals, butterflies, old maps (from books or drawings), and old art pictures. (Museum catalogs have beautiful pictures and you can get them by writing to the museum in your area. The Metropolitan Museum in New York City will send a lovely, slick

A purse made for me by James Hutchins of Raleigh, N.C. The Hummel prints came from Christmas cards. *Photo by Ross Chapple*

67

A purse made by James Hutchins using a bought print, "Castle and Stage Coach." *Photo by Ross Chapple*

A variety of purses made by James Hutchins. *Photo by Ross Chapple*

Decoupage on wood. *Photo by Ross Chapple*

69

catalog to you for 75 cents.) Collect any pretty pictures you come across on postcards, Christmas cards, calendars, seed catalogs, magazines, fancy candy boxes, or any other available source.

Select the ones you want to decoupage, but make sure they're not pictures that were reproduced poorly, for too much time goes into a decoupage project to use inferior materials. You may use color or black and white or you may even color your own prints (such as a coloring book or a paint-by-number picture). Oil-based pencils give you richer color tones than watercolor ones. Good crayons with an oily base are effective too. You may color all the cutouts you use, giving your project a very personal touch, or you may highlight colored cutouts from magazines or cards with acrylic paint, touching up the spots you want to emphasize. Remember you will need borders, trims, and connecting pieces for your pictures, so collect these as well.

Materials

A collection of good pictures, borders, trims, and connecting pieces
Curved scissors (cuticle type)
Glue (Elmer's is fine or any other transparent glue that is water soluble when used but not when dry. Glue should dry quickly, but not immediately, so you can move your pictures.)
Container for glue and water. It's easier to work with glue that has been squeezed into a small cup.
Small brush for gluing
Sponge to smooth out pictures and remove excess glue
Lintless cloth
Tape measure to measure surfaces to be covered and pictures to fit
Ruler
Varnish or lacquer
Brush for varnishing (small)
Turpentine or mineral spirits
Sealer
Sandpaper (fine)
Steel wool (0000 grade) to clean sanded surfaces to remove all dust and loose particles.
Wax or finishing compound

Directions

Clean the object to be decoupaged thoroughly. It is of the utmost importance that the object be clean, smooth, and dry. If you're going to work on wood, clean it thoroughly. When it's completely dry, sand it lightly. Paint or stain the wood at this point, if you wish. Unseasoned (green) wood must have a coat of sealer, if it is to be used in its natural state. After the sealer has dried, sand the piece again, lightly. Rough wood must be sanded smooth, if you want cutouts to stick to it smoothly. The surface of any wood must be smooth. If it has been painted unevenly, all paint lumps must be sanded out.

Old metal pieces must be sanded with sandpaper to make the surface smooth. If it has peeling paint, remove the paint with paint remover before sanding.

Glass or ceramic pieces take decoupage best when they have been wiped off with denatured alcohol and sprayed with one or two coats of sealer before gluing.

All cutouts to be used on a single piece must be the same thickness. If you want to combine picture-card thickness with magazine thickness, you must peel the thicker pieces. This may be done in two ways: With the first method, moisten the back of the picture with white vinegar. Use just enough to coat it, but not to wet it through. Let it set for a few minutes and rub the back gently with your finger or a damp cloth, until the back either peels or rubs off. Working gently with this process, bring your cutout to the same thickness of the other prints to be used. It's wise to spray the front of the cutout with sealer so that it retains its shape and does not wrinkle.

With the second method you spray the cutout first, then soak it for about ten minutes in lukewarm water. Usually, you can peel the back off in layers. By spraying sealer on the picture before soaking, the picture won't run or fade.

Experiment in arranging your designs. Place them in various ways to create the most pleasing effect. Cut each piece so that it fits its neighbor properly. When you are satisfied with your layout, you're ready to glue.

We have used Elmer's glue effectively. Pour the glue into a small cup; then apply it sparingly with a brush. Excess glue will lump under your picture. If the glue is too thick, add a few drops of water for thinning. A small roller is invaluable for rolling over the cutout surface, pushing out all air bubbles, and spreading the glue underneath evenly.

Everybody will have a different method of placing their cutouts on the object being decorated. A friend of mine uses a spot of glue (put on with the tip of a toothpick) to hold the cutouts in place and lays the whole picture in sort of a dry run for effect. Others use Plasti-Tak which will peel away easily. If the surface is flat, you will have no trouble doing a layout; it's as easy as putting a puzzle together. Depending on what your project is, you will figure out the best way to lay out your finished picture.

If you find that an old trunk which you wish to decoupage or line with newsprint is musty smelling, there are two ways to make it smell clean and sweet. One is to give it a coat of white shellac; the other is to put several pieces of charcoal inside and close the lid. Leave it closed for several days and, usually, the musty smell goes away.

Eighteenth-century craftsmen used lacquer on their imitations of Japanese and Chinese objects, but for the amateur, lacquers are difficult to apply. They are quick-drying, but so are clear, satin finishes; the latter are much easier to apply. I sometimes thin the finish with a paint thinner, so that coats are very light. Many pieces require as many as thirty or forty coats to build up a smooth, glossy "hand-painted" look. It's important that each coat of finish dry thoroughly before another coat is applied. The length of time depends on the finish used. Quick-drying finishes may be completely dry in four hours, but for the best results I like to leave my work overnight before sanding and applying another coat. When you run your hand over the surface, it should feel so smooth that you cannot feel where the application of cutouts are. After each coat, when the finish is dry, sand lightly. Make sure there are no bubbles or rough spots. On very small objects, you can use the spray finishes in a can. These, however, are more expensive, and the effect not as transparently glossy as hand-applied finish. It's the build-up of finish that makes your pieces beautiful and professional looking.

If you decide you'd like to go into advanced (museum quality) decoupage, one of the most complete books on the market today is *Contemporary Decoupage* by Thelma R. Newman (Crown Publishers, New York, New York, 1972; $7.95).

12

Potichomania:
Gluing Paper Cutouts to Glass

THE word "potichomania" is derived from *"potiche,"* a French word meaning porcelain vase, according to the 1880 edition of Merriam-Webster's dictionary. Potichomania, apparently, is not an ancient art, for *Godey's Lady's Book* for January 1855 was the first publication to give directions for what it called "this new mode of ornamenting"—a process of ornamenting vases and other glassware. The magazine article

Potichomania vases and ornaments illustrated in *Peterson's Magazine,* June 1860.

73

stressed the fact that the art had become a rage in Paris and would probably become popular in America, which it did. I imagine that one of the reasons for its popularity was that the art required no talent or knowledge of drawing or painting.

Materials

Glass vases in shapes suitable to be decorated
Sheets of colored drawings or prints, sizes and shapes to fit vases
White glue (Elmer's)
3 or 4 (¼- to ½-inch) paint brushes
Fine-pointed scissors for cutting out designs
An assortment of quick-drying enamel paints for foundation
Glass container for mixing and diluting paints
Gold paint for decorating borders
Varnish (clear and quick-drying) for sealer on finished piece

Many department stores, five-and-ten stores, and supermarkets sell plain glass vases (often called crystal) for very little. Wide-mouth vases or jars are the easiest to work with, for you can get your hand inside to arrange your design. Experiment with gluing pictures to plain glass before embarking on the real potichomania. Some glues work better on some papers than others. I used Elmer's glue, diluted 1 part glue to 1 part water. It worked very well, but there are many other glues on the market that work satisfactorily. Generally speaking, a glue should be transparent, nonstaining, and water-soluble when put on but not when dried. It should take a few minutes to dry, so that you have time to move or adjust your design. Always keep a damp sponge ready to press over your picture and absorb all the surplus glue. Make sure that the edges of your design stick tightly, so that paint poured into the vase does not seep in around your design.

Directions

If you decide to imitate a Chinese vase, you must select your prints—those that will give your vase a Chinese look. Cut them out accurately with a pair of scissors, and arrange them as you wish. Apply glue with a brush to the face side of prints (the colored side) and place them to the inside of the vase, glued side against glass. Press down with a damp sponge, smoothing out all air bubbles. Make sure the prints adhere closely to the glass.

When the prints have had sufficient time to dry, use your glue brush and cover every part of them on the back with glue (without touching the glass) and allow to dry. This prevents the base oil color (which is next applied) from sinking into or becoming absorbed by the paper prints.

Select the base color you want to use on your vase. Pour the paint into a glass container. If it appears to be too thick to pour smoothly, dilute it gradually with paint thinner until a smooth-flowing consistency is attained.

Now pour the contents of the container into the vase. Hold the vase in both hands and turn it around continually in the same direction, until the color is spread equally and evenly over the inside of the vase. Pour the surplus paint back into the glass container. When the paint inside the vase is completely dry, pour clear varnish or sealer into the vase and repeat the turning procedure until the inside surface is coated. Pour out surplus and allow the vase to dry completely. The mouth of the vase may be decorated with gold paint, if desired; then varnish it.

Pairs of potichomania vases make beautiful lamp bases. There is no limit to the things you can make by this process and any one of them, well-done, will become an heirloom you will treasure and be proud to pass on to your children.

If you want to practice on a bottle, before buying a vase, here is an easy way to cut the top off a bottle:

Remove all labels and glue from the bottle. Clean it and let it dry thoroughly. A wet bottle will not do. Tie yarn around the bottle at the point you want to sever. Saturate with alcohol. Set fire to the yarn and when it is almost completely burned around the bottle, dip the bottle into a bucket of cold water. This should break the bottle at that point, unless the glass is too thick, in which case, repeat the process.

13

Velvet Painting and Appliqués

VELVET PAINTING

The term *velvet painting* does not necessarily mean painting on velvet. Velvet painting is applying paint to fabric—any fabric. Back in the eighteenth century, the Chinese painted on a material made from wood pulp that had been pounded to paper thinness, giving off a velvet-like appearance. Perhaps that is where the name "velvet painting" received its name. However, many beautiful paintings on velvet itself have found their way into museums and antiques shops. There were others done on satins and silks that were just as beautiful and modern ways of velvet painting include doing them on muslins and heavy cotton materials as well. You can do velvet painting even if you have no artistic talent at all. It is simple and there are many variations and methods of doing it today.

I have found muslin the easiest fabric to work with. A picture on muslin takes on a canvas-like appearance, and muslin can be tinted any color you want. Cut your muslin the size of the frame to be used. You may tack it to a board, tape it to heavy cardboard or, if a small picture is planned, use a regular embroidery hoop to hold the fabric taut.

Embroidery transfers are ideal for beginners. The popular basket-and-flowers used so often on pillowcases and scarves makes a lovely, easy-to-paint design. Both the hot iron and the tracing transfers are easy to do. Make sure the design is centered on your material. You may

76

Painting of flowers on muslin. *Photo by Ross Chapple*

add petals falling from the basket or other designs in addition to your basket.

Once the design that you're going to paint is transferred to material, spray a thin coat of sealer over the entire fabric. This prevents any of your colors from running. When dry, paint, choosing colors as you would select thread for embroidering. Regular artists' oil paints, which may be bought in small tubes, are ideal for painting, but you may want to experiment with oil crayons or watercolors as well. Allow the finished picture to dry thoroughly and then apply another coat of sealer.

APPLIQUÉS

Appliqué velvet painting is fun for the whole family. You may cut out designs from paper or materials and glue them onto fabric with 3M wood and paper glue. You may use one of the many colorful prints on the market today. If the print is the right size and the material it is on is heavy enough, you may use the material in lieu of muslin and simply paint over the printed design.

If you decide to use smaller cutouts from material, glue them in place on your muslin. After your picture has been glued on, simply paint over it, using the same colors of the cutout or new colors, as you wish. The overall result is fantastic, and no one would suspect that you had used such a pattern to paint because the glued-on prints will be completely covered with paint and will not show through.

Paper prints may be glued on the same way. Let's say you find a pretty paper basket in a magazine which you wish to use. You could then add the flowers or fruits from cloth prints. There is no limit to what you can do, and the fact that you have no talent for drawing will not prevent you from making a beautiful velvet painting that will certainly be an heirloom to pass on to your children.

14

Painting on Wood

PAINTING on wood is one of the easiest crafts to do, for it doesn't necessarily require artistic talent. Designs may be traced or stenciled, and if your painting looks amateurish, it doesn't matter because most wood paintings are primitive and almost anything is acceptable.

The first step, of course, is selecting your wood. Having been associated with antiques for so long, I love old woods—the kinds that have mellowed with years of age and exposure to the elements—old barrel tops, cheese boxes, the fronts of old drawers (where a chest or table has been damaged beyond repair), old doors, shingles, or scrap pieces of wood that you may find in the trash or in somebody's back yard. The trash of a second-hand store is a gold mine for paintable material. The backs or arms of demolished antique chairs make unusual bases for wood paintings. If you have difficulty finding old wood, settle for bread boards or cutting boards that may be purchased for very little; or use pieces of new wood, which you can treat to look old.

I was first attracted to wood paintings when I stopped in a Holiday Inn that had the dining-room walls covered with huge wood paintings. They gave the interior an atmosphere of an old tavern. The paintings were of an historical nature: Indians, men on horseback, soldiers, and the like. The effect was outstanding, and I was so fascinated that I returned home and decided to try to make a wood painting of my own. I discovered it was not too difficult and the possibilities were unlimited.

Pair of historical wood paintings by Virginia Warren. *Photo by Ross Chapple*

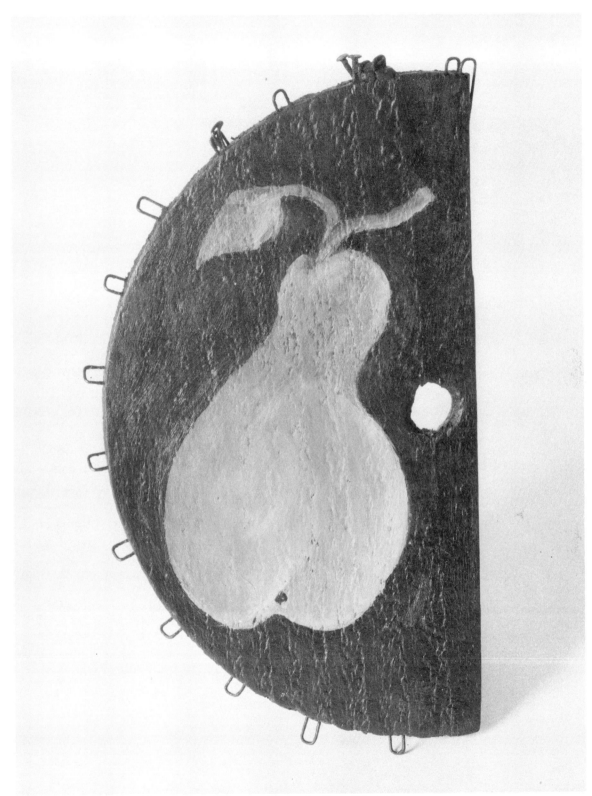

Painting on old keg lid by Virginia Warren. *Photo by Ross Chapple*

81

PASS IT ON

Outside of the paints, you probably have all the materials you need in your kitchen.

Materials

Clorox
Vinegar
Knox gelatin
Regular carbon paper
White carbon paper (the kind used in sewing, may be purchased from sewing center)
Picture-hanging hooks
Paints (tubes of oil or acrylic or small bottles of model plane or car enamel)
Small artists' brushes
Fine sandpaper

Directions

Prepare your wood. If the wood is too dark, bleach it with several washes of undiluted Clorox. If the wood is too light and you want it darkened, wash several times with undiluted vinegar. If the wood is too rough, sand to smoothness desired.

Place one envelope of gelatin in a cup of water and rub the wood over with it. When dry, repeat. This seals the wood so that your paints will not soak into it. When dry, you are ready to trace on your design.

If the wood is dark, use white carbon paper; if light, use dark.

You can select your designs from newspaper pictures, coloring books, magazines, posters, or cards. Almost any picture can be traced. If the picture is in a book, trace onto clear paper and then on the wood.

Oil paints take longer to dry than the others mentioned. Acrylics dry almost instantly, as do the model-car enamels.

Have fun. Make a wood painting for every member of your family. Select designs that they will like. Remember, you can make greeting cards on small shingles or pieces of wood and place cards for special occasions, like weddings, birthdays, or any memorable day in the life of your family. These are the type of things that become heirlooms, to be treasured forever.

15

Wood Whittling

MANY of our most valuable antiques were either "whittled" or carved by hand. There is something very special about a piece of wood that has been shaped and finished by hand. In the old days, there were special wood-carvers who did nothing else. If an ordinary citizen decided to make a piece of furniture, and wanted carving in places, he might send it to one of these wood-carvers, who would follow his instructions and carve the piece.

This chapter is about things you can whittle out of wood, even if you haven't a woodworking tool in the house. Professionals, who have woodworking shops in their basements or garages, will have their own patterns for pieces, but the pieces I describe here are for "whittlers" who enjoy cutting things out with a pocketknife or kitchen paring knife.

My grandfather was a great whittler. He enjoyed taking a stick and turning it into something useful with his pocketknife. Even the toys he made for his grandchildren were not frivolous and could be put to some other use. The little rocker he made for me doubled as a sewing cabinet, and it is one of the most treasured possessions I have. The pattern is simple and the finished piece requires no nails, only glue. The pattern I have drawn is the size of my rocker but I am sure that you can make it any size you want by drawing your own pattern.

83

Rocker made by my grandfather. *Photo by Ross Chapple*

ROCKER

Lay a piece of thin paper (onionskin or tissue) over the patterns and trace. Use carbon paper and trace your pattern onto cardboard. Cut out the pattern from cardboard and you will have a permanent pattern to keep. You may want to make cardboard furniture from the same pattern sometime.

Trace pattern onto piece of wood about ¼–½ inch in thickness. You will need two pieces for the sides of rocker.

84

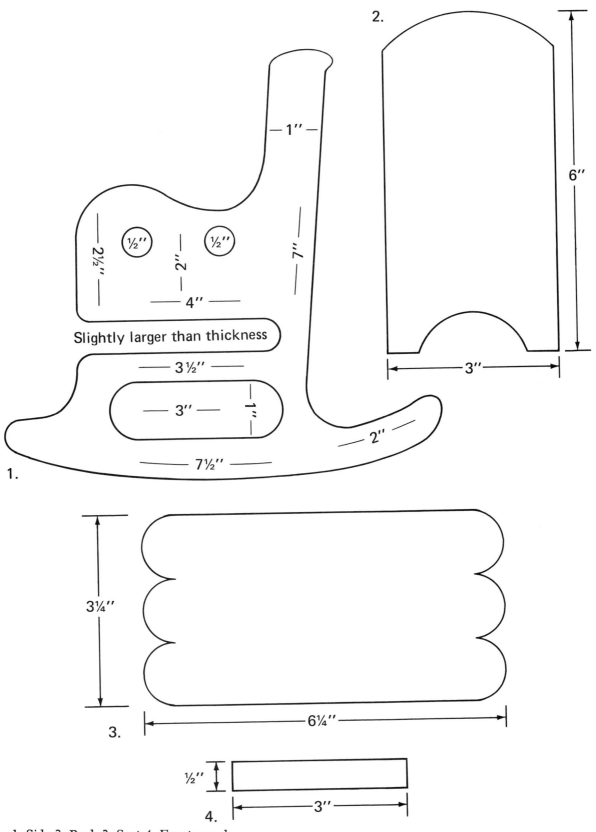

2.

6″

3″

1″

½″ ½″

2½″ 2″ 7″

4″

Slightly larger than thickness

3½″

3″ 1″

7½″

2″

1.

3¼″

6¼″

3.

½″

3″

4.

1. Side 2. Back 3. Seat 4. Front panel

PASS IT ON

Cut by paring away the wood a little at a time until desired shape is achieved. Slide the seat piece into slot in chair sides. Fit back in place, letting it tilt in to meet the seat. Now that you have seen how it fits, you're ready to start gluing. Using quick-drying cement glue such as Duro contact cement, coat inside slot that seat fits into and around the sides of back panel. Fit back together again and clamp the two sides firmly against the back. If you haven't a clamp, put strong rubber bands around the chair until completely dry. If you want to use thin nails on the sides of chair, you may, but it is not necessary. In later years, when the glue on my chair became loose, I did nail it in places, rather than take the chair apart and re-glue it.

When the chair is dry, coat three edges of the front panel with glue and slip into place in slot in front of chair.

If you want to make a sewing chair, as mine is, before gluing the chair together, drive three nails (large ones) through the ends of the seat board to hold spools of thread and, using wire cutters, snip off the pointed tops.

My chair is of plywood with clear shellac on it. You may finish your chair any way you want, even paint it if your wood is not particularly pretty.

LITTLE HANGING SHELF

I made this little shelf to hold a miniature kettle set that one of my daughters won in a contest. The shelf alone would have little value as an heirloom, but put together with some little treasure, it becomes an attractive combination. The kettles and pots and pans were so tiny

Easy-to-make hanging shelf. *Photo by Ross Chapple*

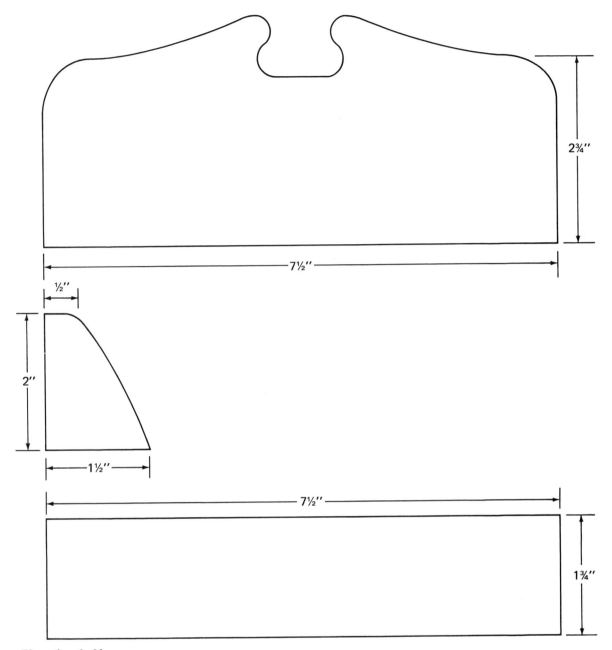

Plans for shelf.

(especially the lids) that I knew they would be lost in no time unless we found a way to keep them intact. I cut this shelf from a cheese box.

I drew my pattern freehand on cardboard. You may trace this one, as you did the chair pattern (see illustration). I like to keep my patterns on cardboard and often spray them with clear varnish so they don't become frayed after many usages.

Trace cardboard patterns on very thin wood (cheese box, cigar box,

87

and so on). Cut out with sharp pocketknife. Smooth out with sandpaper.

I brush the glue on where the pieces fit, then use two thin picture-frame nails on each side of back where shelf meets side. Screw little hooks into the front to hold kettles.

Spray clear varnish if you want a natural finish; or stain, as I did, then varnish when the stain is dry. I rubbed the stain on with a rag and wiped off immediately. That way I can control how much I use.

This little shelf is ideal for dollhouses or play areas. Later on, when your children are grown, it makes a lovely kitchen decoration.

There are so many things you can "whittle." Not many people do it anymore, but I'm sure you'll find it's fun to do, and all you need is a good pocketknife and lots of patience. Try making patterns of your own for many different things. Save shirt boards from the laundry; they're ideal for patterns. With the new miracle glues, such as Crazy Glue or contact cement, that are on the market today, you can make almost anything without hammer and nails.

16

Dollhouses and Miniature Doll Furniture

COLLECTING dollhouses and miniature furniture is said to be the third largest hobby in the country today. Dollhouses often become heirlooms, and are passed down from mother to daughter to granddaughter. The scope of designs, sizes, and quality are so far-reaching that you might collect a hundred and have no two alike—there are dollhouses and dollhouses. Some are made from packing boxes or cardboard cartons; some made them from wood and with such exquisite detail and labor that they rank with museum pieces. The first group of houses were made to play with; the latter as creative art works to be admired and cherished for a lifetime.

Colleen Moore, the movie actress, traveled the country for years with her dollhouse called "The Castle," which was worth a million dollars in 1935. In her little house, the library held miniature editions of classics edited especially for the dollhouse. Among her many tiny books was an abridged version of *This Side of Paradise* with these lines by F. Scott Fitzgerald: "I was the spark that lit up Flaming Youth; Colleen Moore was the torch."

Queen Mary of England had a beautiful dollhouse which was designed by Sir Edwin Lutyens and made by some of her loyal subjects. In the Victorian era, many architects built "sample" miniature houses,

89

The interior of a Michigan house in miniature. *Courtesy the Washington Dolls' House and Toy Museum*

exactly like the main house would be, to make sure it pleased the buyer. The Smithsonian Institution in Washington, D.C., has one such house.

So popular are dollhouses with adults, that one master craftsman, Marion Howes, a seventy-eight-year-old retired electrician, who makes about six or seven dollhouses a year, claims he makes them mostly for grown women and once in a while for their teen-age daughters. Mr. Howes is a master at his craft; he works out every possible detail. One house he built for a customer was patterned after a New England colonial his customer found in a paint catalog. The dollhouse had 2,400 cedar shake shingles on its roof, birch floors, mahogany paneling, a solid chestnut staircase with turned posts, a beamed ceiling, and handmade brass door knobs. It was wired for electricity with copper strands hidden between the ceiling and floorboards and was completely insulated so that the wires did not touch wood in any place.

If you would like to contact a dollhouse builder in your area, you might write to *The Nutshell News*, La Jolla, California, or the *International Doll's House News*, Sussex, England. These publications report regularly on builders all over.

The reason I tell you about the dollhouse craftsmen is two-fold: You may be interested in having your dollhouse built for you to house the miniature furniture that you build yourself, or you may receive expert advice and knowledge by visiting a builder in your area. All dollhouse plans are different, and I'm sure no two builders will construct their houses the same way.

So popular is miniature doll furniture that new specialty shops are springing up all over the country. In Northern Virginia, I visited a shop which had a small handmade sofa (carved of wood) with cushions. They were asking $56 for the sofa, while a matching chair sold for $39. I was told that before Christmas, their stock was almost depleted, so there is a market for these expensive little pieces. The most expensive line of miniature furniture is made by Chestnut Hill. One of their leather wing chairs brings $50; a Duncan Phyfe sofa is $75.

You can get almost anything in miniature: There are tiny playing cards, clocks, newspapers (a *New York Times* that can be read with a magnifying glass), doll electric hair dryers, typewriters, and electric organs (selling for $160). It's expensive to buy any of them, but from ordinary "trash-can-candidates" (things you throw away every day) it's possible to make delightful dollhouse settings and furnishings. Broken jewelry, buttons, coke caps, champagne wires, pill bottles, toothpaste caps, berry cartons, scraps of felt or carpeting, and small strong cardboard boxes (the type perfume is packed in) can be turned into beautiful bed-

91

Exterior of York, Pennsylvania townhouse, second half of the nineteenth century. *Photo courtesy of Flora Gill Jacobs*

rooms, living rooms, Spanish patio bedrooms, and old-fashioned kitchens.

A whole house full of miniature doll furniture can be made without driving a nail—you need use only a clear household cement such as Duro contact cement, bottles of model-car enamel, and bits and pieces of things you throw away every day. Wooden crates in which fruits are shipped to the grocery store make ideal rooms to house the furniture and knick-knacks. I won't even mention the pleasure you'll derive from being creative. You'll be achieving something different, something that is hard to find and expensive when you do find it. Miniature furniture is almost impossible to find in stores (except in specialty shops), and when you do find a piece, you pay an exorbitant price for it and chances are it's plastic and unattractive.

Egg cartons can be converted into many basic pieces of furniture. They are easy to upholster and, when coated with enamel, become hard and durable. Matchboxes (the penny size) make beautiful desks, vanities, and chests. If you are lucky enough to come across the older wood matchboxes, by all means, hold on to them for they are priceless in making miniature furniture.

Never buy the large sizes of paints (except for painting the walls of a room). Inexpensive bottles of model-car enamels are perfect for this hobby. They have the high gloss of Chinese enamel and come in a great range of colors. A tiny bottle goes a long way on small pieces of furniture.

Once you get into making miniature furniture, you'll never throw anything away. Corks, the ordinary kind that come on many bottles, can be cut for bricks and painted to look like a realistic fireplace. Drinking straws, laid out side-by-side and glued together make a roof for your house, a carpet for your floor, or a colorful screen to divide rooms. Copper wiring can be woven into an "antique brass" headboard for a doll bed.

Doll rooms in these enchanting "small world" sizes definitely have an heirloom quality about them. As gifts, they will warm the heart of any little girl and be treasured for many years. Your own child will never cease to wonder how you were able to put together such a charming house from bits and pieces. She'll most likely want to save it for her own little girl. Then too, they bring fantastic prices at bazaars and fund-raising sales.

Prepare your rooms first. The size of the furniture you make will depend on the size of the room you select. If wooden boxes are not available, select heavy cardboard ones for your first venture. Decide whether you want to paper or paint your walls. Leave one side open, so

Reproduction of a 1735 general store and post office in Virginia. *Photo courtesy of Flora Gill Jacobs*

94

that you can see into the room. Then again, do you want to carpet or paint the floor? Decide where you want the windows to go and where the fireplace goes, if you want one.

If wooden crates are used for a room, turn the crates on their sides and look for picture frames (plain wooden ones) that fit the opening. If you can't find ready-made ones, have a frame made, for a glass-enclosed room is much more valuable and the glass protects the furnishings. Try to get several boxes the same size so they will stack one on top of the other. If you have side-by-side rooms, they are most attractive placed on wall brackets which you may buy for very little in five-and-ten stores and hardware stores.

WALLS

Paint or paper the walls. If paint is used, make sure the color is bright and cheerful but not overwhelming. If paper is used, make sure the pattern is small. Let your imagination take you on a voyage of discovery. Decorate the walls the way you like: curtains, drapes, or a mixture of paper and paint. Wallpaper stores will give you books of outdated patterns if you ask for them. A little warning here: If you select wallpaper, make sure you leave one wall bare to be painted, so you can hang all those lovely little delft plates and mirrors and other whatnots you'll be making. All curtains and draperies may be glued (hems and tops) with rubber cement or Elmer's, unless you prefer sewing them.

Two small brass hooks (the kind you hang cups on in a cupboard), a pencil (painted gold), and a bottle cork, cut in half and painted gold, give you all the fixtures you need for hanging draperies. Screw the hook (for each side of window) into the painted cork and glue the cork to the wall in the proper place. A new pencil, painted gold, makes an ideal curtain rod and will fit nicely into the hooks.

FLOORS

Floors may be laid of tiny bathroom tiles, pieces of felt, linoleum, or carpeting, which may be glued to the floor of the room. If you feel industrious, you can paint the floors and use little handmade scatter rugs, which you may make from braiding knitting yarn or small cotton strips.

FURNITURE

Sofa. Cut the end of an egg carton top, approximately 1 inch from end. This part will give you the frame for the seat, back, and arms

95

which should be painted or upholstered. You may attach legs by gluing on bottle caps or sticks of wood with Elmer's, or you may cut an identical piece from the other end of the carton, turn it upside-down with the opening to the back, and glue the soft part to this inverted base. You could cover the base with a ruffle. To upholster, simply glue on velvet ribbon. Fit with cushions.

Chair. The egg "cups," which hold the eggs in the carton, are naturals for chair frames. Trim around an egg cup, cutting low in front for the front of the seat; cut a little higher for the arms and much higher for the back. To make it a modern chair, simply glue on a painted bottle cap at the bottom; for an antique chair, use painted matchsticks for the legs, and upholster the chair in velvet by gluing on velvet ribbon. A cushion will fill the egg cup to the level of the seat.

Tester bed. This bed requires the 4 ends of two egg cartons. Cut each one 2½ inches from the end. Invert 2 ends and glue together, overlapping slightly. This makes the bed frame. Cut 4 dowel sticks or popsicle sticks 4 inches long. If dowels are used, glue them to the top four corners of the bed frame. If popsicle sticks are used, glue to sides of bed frame. Glue the other two carton ends the same way you did the bed frame. Trim ½ inch off the sides. Invert and place on top of posts and glue. This makes the base for the canopy. Glue a ruffle around the bed frame. Make a mattress the size of the bed and place it on the bed. Bed posts may be painted or stained. The canopy should be ruffled with frilly material (organdy or the like) and glued to carton top.

FURNITURE FROM ODDS AND ENDS

Sofa from a box. Select a sturdy, cardboard box the size of the sofa desired. Turn the box upside down, then take the box lid, invert it and glue it back-to-back to the bottom of box. The openings are now top and bottom. Cut the apron off the front of the top, leaving apron around the sides and back for arms and back of sofa. If the apron is high, you may cut down the arms to be lower than the back. Upholster the whole sofa in velvet ribbon, which is much easier to glue on than material. Add "embroidery" by gluing on little rosettes around the bottom. Covered buttons make sofa pillows of contrasting velvet.

Tester bed. Following the egg-crate tester bed, you may use any box (the right size) of strong construction (such as perfume-bottle box, soap box, or gift box) whose lid has a small apron. Separate the top from bottom. Give both parts two coats of enamel, along with four posts (dowel pins, squared sticks, or popsicle sticks) cut to the desired height.

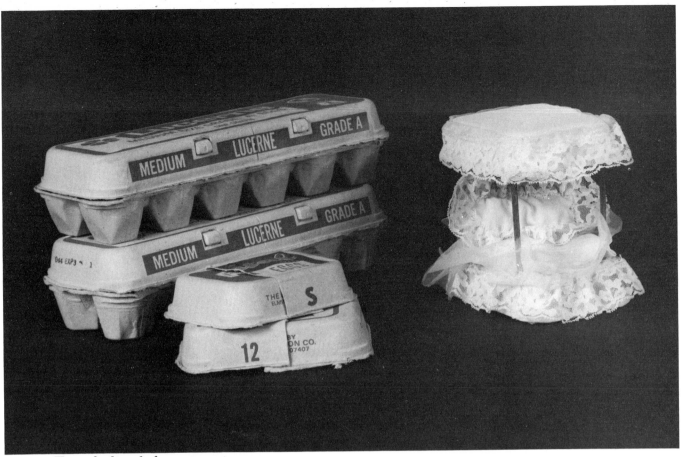

Tester bed made from egg carton.

Desk made from penny match boxes.

PASS IT ON

Glue the four posts to the corners of the inverted box base. Glue the top of the posts to the box cover, which sits, apron side down on the posts. Allow it to dry thoroughly. Glue ruffles of organdy and lace into place. (Bobby pins make fine supports to hold material in place until the glue dries.) Velvet ribbon is used as a border. If you prefer, you may sew the coverlet with contrasting-colored velvet.

Desk. Eight penny boxes of matches supply the sides and drawers of your kneehole desk. A flatter matchbox works as the center, which is the connecting link. Paint all the boxes (black is a good color for the desk) and, after two coats of enamel, stack and glue 4 boxes for either side, so that drawers will open. Then glue the center drawer to the top drawers of these stacks as shown in illustration. If you like the Oriental effect, sprinkle mother-of-pearl over small dabs of glue. (Mother-of-pearl is made from crushing pearl buttons.) Handles for drawers may be any number of ornamental things, such as buttons, thumbtacks, or little brass bolts slipped through washers, pushed through the front of drawers, and nutted on the inside.

Grandfather clock. Glue together three small matchboxes, enamel them mahogany-brown, and trim with gold braid. Cut the face from a clock picture in a magazine, glue it on, and circle it with the gold-finished ring from an earring. Then hang gold threads from the clock face and top it off with brass heads of tacks. (This makes the pendulum.)

Egg carton sofa and chair.

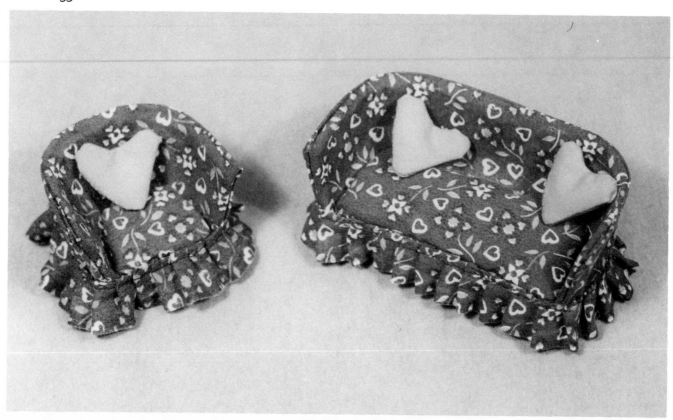

Vanity. This is made like the desk, but it's antiqued in white and gold. A compact mirror, edged with gold braid or brass frame, hangs over it.

Chairs. There are several kinds of chairs one can make: Occasional chairs (large coat buttons, covered in velvet, and laid on champagne-wire circles with wire legs which have been painted gold) or heavy chairs made the same as the sofas but from smaller boxes (ring boxes). Backs of the occasional chairs can be made of wire (painted gold), with butterfly appliqués glued on. The heavy chairs can be upholstered as the sofas are.

Tables. A console table can be made from an anchovy can, enameled, and trimmed with gold. Legs may be fan spokes or popsicle sticks, also painted gold. Kitchen tables can be made from inverted box lids (enameled) glued to dowel legs and occasional tables from small metal lids (from jars) mounted over thread spools and enameled. Large thread spools, painted white, and with gingham cushions (covered buttons) make ideal kitchen stools.

KNICK-KNACKS

Buttons and pieces of costume jewelry may be used in many ways. Buttons, painted and decorated, become plates to hang on the wall; a sunburst pin, with the face of a clock cemented to the middle, becomes a decorator's clock. A twig, painted and glued to the middle of the wall of the bathroom, makes a towel rack on which you can hang little towels. A mascara brush becomes a fireplace broom. Small deodorant jars make beautiful flowerpots. Mother-of-pearl buttons make candle holders, to which a birthday candle is attached. Small pictures, clipped from magazines and framed (in earring hoops), make pretty pictures for the wall.

17

Heirloom Dolls to Make

THE most valued dolls are not always the fine bisque and porcelain ones that were purchased for us by our parents. More often the home-made stuffed dolls, those carved out of wood or fashioned from corn husks were the ones that comforted us as children and became the great treasures from our childhood. For this reason, I think every child should have a handmade doll—made especially for her. The following dolls are just a few that any parent can make easily, inexpensively, and in a very short time.

OLD-FASHIONED APPLE DOLL

Materials

1 large round, hard unripe apple for the head
2 whole cloves or other small, dark objects that will stick into an apple for eyes
Knitting yarn for hair and for padding
1 8-inch styrofoam Christmas tree form (cone shaped) or the padded cylinder from a roll of toilet paper, for the torso
¼ yard of calico or light-colored cotton fabric for the dress
Ribbon for the trim
1 cup vinegar or lemon juice for apple dipping
Rubber cement

100

Directions

Core and peel the apple. Dip the apple in the vinegar or lemon juice. Lightly carve eyes, nose, mouth, cheeks, and chin with a teaspoon, keeping them well apart because the apple will shrink to less than half its original size. Stud the eye sockets with cloves, setting them in deep.

Set the head on a stick or dowel so that air can reach inside the cored part. Keep uncovered in a dry place, away from anything that might bruise it and make the apple rot. In about two weeks, the apple will dry to a leathery hardness that looks like carved wood.

Meanwhile, thread a pipe cleaner carefully through the top of the

Apple dolls by Mrs. Ganell Marshall. Bodies made from cornhusks, cleaned and dyed. *Photo courtesy Appalachian Spring, Washington, D.C.*

101

styrofoam cone or torso, about an inch or more below the tip, to form the arms. Cover the arms generously with rubber cement and then pad them with knitting wool by wrapping it around. Repeat the wrapping process on the torso.

Cut two oblong strips, 1½ inches square and ¼ inch thick from another hard apple and allow them to dry overnight or longer. When firm, yet pliable, cut two hands with the fingers parted. Let them dry and then glue them to the pipe cleaner with rubber cement.

Body may be made from cornhusks as well. Just follow directions from cornhusk doll.

To make the dress, cut fabric into four strips: 9-by-18 inches for the skirt; 5-by-7 inches for the bodice; and two strips, 4-by-6 inches for the sleeves, to be sewn lengthwise.

Draw sleeves over padded arms and sew or glue to top of cone (or other torso). Fold bodice strip crosswise. Cut small shallow opening for neck. Sew a slantwise tuck from neck to shoulders on the wrong side. Put the dress on doll. Fold the fabric under itself for capped-sleeve effect and fasten under the arms.

Make a 2-inch hem at the bottom of the skirt, and sew a casing at the top for ⅜-inch elastic; put tiny hook and eye at the ends. Sew the back seam. Trim hem with ribbon.

To assemble, glue yarn to apple head for wig; attach head to cone with a long straight pin concealed under the hair or glue it in place to the torso. Eyeglasses, which are optional, are made from strands of picture-frame wire. As the apple shrinks, the skin seems to form eyelids.

There are many variations of dressing the dolls. Bottles may be used for the torso, if you have a shape that an apple will fit. For men or boy dolls, legs of carved soap, wood, or clay may be used, so the doll can be fitted with pants. Pants can be made by cutting out a triangle (wide end at the bottom edge and centered) from two squares of material. Sew the outside and inside seams; hem the legs; and encase a bit of elastic at the top for a snug waist. Experiment. Rice serves as teeth, if the doll's mouth is open. Finished dolls may be mounted on small boards so they stand erect.

CORNHUSK DOLLS

Legend has it that the Indians taught the Pilgrims to make the first cornhusk dolls, but the Americans are accredited with putting faces on the dolls. Some Indian superstitions forbade putting a face on any doll, lest the doll take on a soul and become filled with evil spirits.

Cornhusk dolls by Mrs. Ganell Marshall. These little people are carefully fashioned from natural cornhusks. *Photo courtesy Appalachian Spring, Washington, D.C.*

To become expert in making cornhusk dolls, one might study *Corn-Husk Crafts* by Margaret Flacklam and Patricia Phibbs (New York: Sterling, 1973) or *Corn Shuck Craft* by Marguerite Cain Crawford (New York: Exposition, 1967). There are many variations, but the basic principle is the same for making any doll.

Children today, as children of old, love these unusual dolls and they're so simple to make. Even if you live in the city and never go near a garden, the ears of fresh corn you buy in the supermarket will supply all the husks you need.

103

Lovely cornhusk
lady and baby.
*Photo courtesy
Appalachian Spring,
Washington, D.C.*

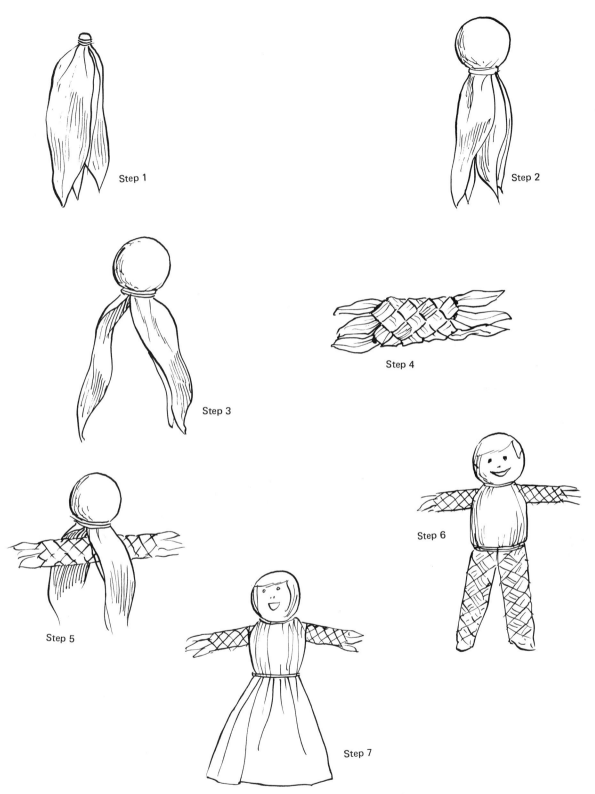

Step 1. Tie shucks together at top. Step 2. Turn inside out, pull shucks down around first tie and retie to make head. Step 3. Divide bottom. Step 4. Braid three more shucks to make arms. Step 5. Insert arms beneath neck. Step 6. Tie waist, divide and braid legs to make boy doll. Step 7. Fluff bottom to make girl doll.

PASS IT ON

Directions

Save all the shucks or husks and corn silks from the corn your family uses. It will take shucks from ten to twelve ears of corn to make a substantial doll. Spread them out to dry for at least two days, although they may be kept indefinitely. Before forming, shucks should be dampened to make them more pliable. Corn silks make nice hair for the dolls.

Select 3 long shucks for the arms. One end of the shuck is heavier than the other, so arrange them with one heavy end and two lighter ends, so the braids will be fairly even. Braid and tie at each end with heavy thread, leaving a little for fingers. If you want more details on the doll, separate the braided ends into five fingers and lacquer each with clear nail polish, so they stay separated.

Following illustration, tie a heavy bunch (enough for one doll) of shucks with heavy string at the top (the heavy and thickest part). Invert bottom part over the top-tied part and tie string around the neck; this leaves a firm rounded ball for the head. Smooth out the face part by wetting the husks, if necessary, to make them more pliable.

Place braided arms through the body husks below neck; then tie the body husks below the arms to make a waist. Braided arms may be wrapped with knitting yarn, if rounded effect is desired. For girl dolls, divide the leftover husks into two sections (top layer and bottom layer) and arrange as skirt, trimming off bottom for length of skirt. If you spread out husk for a flowing skirt, you can glue the sections together. For a boy doll, divide the bottom husks into two sections and braid them for legs, or they too may be wrapped with yarn for a rounded effect. Small pieces of wood, glued on, make feet.

Face can be "painted" with liquid make-up. Allow the husks to dry thoroughly; then use crayons, paint, or glued-on felt to make eyes, nose, and mouth. Yarn, stitched across the top of the head, makes hair.

These dolls can be dressed in doll clothes made of material, if desired. There are unlimited ways to change the character of the dolls. Experimenting is the best way to find the ones that please you.

"ME" DOLL

No doll will touch the heart of a little boy or girl as much as the "Me" doll. This is a personal, life-size stuffed doll that can wear the youngster's own clothing. Children can participate in planning, making, and dressing the doll, and, because the doll is a replica of the child, every child will treasure it.

106

"Me" doll.

Directions

On newspaper or wrapping paper, lay your child on the floor and trace him with his arms outstretched and legs apart.

Using this pattern, cut out a double layer of muslin.

Machine-stitch the muslin on the wrong side, reverse, and leave an opening on the side of the doll for stuffing.

Stuff with cotton, foam, rags, or nylon hose. Pack the doll until it is taut enough to stand erect.

Let the child help paint on the face, after outline of nose, mouth and

107

eyes have been lightly marked in with pencil. Rouge the cheeks. Use watercolors or oil paints for eyes, eyebrows, and mouth. Use two dots for the nose.

Use knitting yarn of the color of the child's own hair. With a large needle, sew on hair across the doll's head and trim in desired style. With girl dolls, the hair may be braided.

Dress doll, including shoes and socks, with child's own clothing.

Embroider the date and the child's name on the doll's foot. This way the child will know in later years that this is how big he was at age five or six or whatever.

The idea for this most lovable doll came from one of my own children who drew herself on brown paper, colored the face and clothing, and then tied the cutout life-size portrait of herself with red ribbon and presented it to me for Christmas. In large scrawling print, she wrote "This is me." When we decided to make a doll, using the cutout as a pattern, she instantly labeled it the "Me" doll.

CLOTHESPIN DOLL

If you've ever visited any of the craft shops in Williamsburg, Virginia, you've seen the adorable clothespin dolls that are made and sold there. A dressed doll may sell for as much as $4 or $5. The Raggedy Ann clothespin doll is perhaps the most popular.

Directions

Use the long, old-fashioned clothespin with a knobby head. Paint a face on the head of the pin, using oil paints. Using Elmer's or rubber cement, glue rug yarn on top of the head for hair. Bore a hole through the clothespin just below head, and insert a pipe cleaner for arms. Cut out outline of shoes from cardboard and paint. Glue to the ends of clothespin.

For girl dolls, cut a strip of material a little over twice as long as the body of the doll. Fold in half and sew up the side seams, leaving small holes for the arms. Puffed sleeves can be made by sewing together two (opposite) edges of a small square, inserting one end into the armhole of the dress and securing it by sewing or gluing. A tiny piece of elastic can be sewn around the inside of the other end to hold the sleeve close to the pipe cleaner. Repeat for the other side.

Boy dolls are not as attractive, but they may be dressed with pants to slide over the two-prong pin. Some boy dolls simply have the clothes painted directly on the clothespin.

18

Treasured Egg-Crafted Heirlooms

EGG-CRAFTING, an art dating back to sixth-century Byzantium, has surfaced in this country as a popular hobby. In 1973, seventy-five egg-craftsmen from all across the nation met in New Carrollton, Maryland, to exhibit collections of hundreds of decorated hen, ostrich, and goose eggs. So outstanding was this exhibit that one masterpiece, "The Last Supper," a hand-painted, sculpted egg by Glenroy Dankel, was priced at $5,000.

"We're all addicts," Dankel said, referring to the other members of "Eggs-Ibit." Egg decorators are truly dedicated to their art. Many of these modern decorators have captured the knack of turning an ordinary egg into an heirloom of lasting beauty. Perhaps the inspiration comes from the early gorgeous Ukranian eggs or the dazzling, opulent, and be-jeweled nineteenth-century eggs of Peter Carl Fabergé which were commissioned by the Russian czar and which are now on display at the Smithsonian Institution in Washington, D.C.

Mrs. Kit Stansbury, Director of Eggs-Ibit, organized the first national egg exhibit in 1971 in Phillipsburg, New Jersey. In an interview with the *Washington Star-News* she said, "The interest in the craft is amazing, but it's understandable because people catch on quickly. Ideas are unlimited, supplies are simple to get at hobby shops, and eggs can be used as decorative objects, Christmas tree ornaments, or to make more original Easter baskets."

109

PASS IT ON

You will find, if you decide to embark on this venture, that there are many different things you can do to an ordinary egg.

There are many ways of crafting eggs. You can leave the egg closed and paint the surface, etch it, or paste on jewels, pieces of lace, or other decorations. Or you may cut a hole in one side of the egg and place in it a miniature scene, giving it a three-dimension stage effect. The more experienced egg-crafter will do the complicated process of opening one side of the egg (like two doors) to give it a real stage-like effect.

EMPTYING AND DRYING EGGSHELLS

Use room-temperature eggs. The larger the egg, the prettier. Use a hatpin or corsage pin to pierce a small hole in the small end of the egg, and a slightly larger hole in the other end. Make sure the pin has broken the yolk. Shake out the egg over a bowl. The contents may be used for making scrambled eggs. Wash out the inside of the egg with cold, running water. Blow into the small hole, and the water will come out of the larger hole. Allow the shell to dry for several hours, shaking occasionally to make sure the surplus water dries out.

DECORATING SHELLS

Take a kitchen matchstick (what we call country matches) and insert the matchstick into the larger end of the egg. (It will fit in the same hole you made for draining.)

Stick the other end of the match stick into the top of an egg carton. This will support your egg while you're decorating it.

Have 6 to 8 colors of hobby enamel. (These come in small bottles and cost less than 50 cents each.) Select bright colors in varying shades, as well as basic dark ones. Gather beads, sequins, lace, embroidery floss, white glue (Elmer's) a small artist's brush, and a hatpin for spreading glue under the beads, laces, and threads.

Prepare the design you want by drawing light lines with a pencil before gluing. It's more fun making your own designs, but you can copy designs you find in magazines or see in exhibits.

Decorating the egg is a delicate operation. When gluing on beads, sequins, etcetera, lightly touch the egg with the hatpin or toothpick barely dipped in glue. Only a drop is needed to hold the decoration.

DIORAMA OR EGGS WITH SCENES INSIDE

Outline the opening on the empty, dry egg with a pencil. Pierce a hole in the center of the outline with a hatpin or a corsage pin. Work-

110

ing from that hole, with a curved manicuring scissors, slowly, cut a tiny bit of shell at a time, until you reach the outline. *Don't* try to cut the whole opening at one cutting. The egg is less likely to break if the cutting is done a little at a time.

There is another way of doing this that works well for some people. With your pin, punch little perforations around the outline (about ⅛ inch apart). Insert the point of your scissors in one hole and carefully cut from hole to hole. This method is quite good for cutting out heart shapes or other odd shapes that are more intricate. Any rough edges around the opening may be covered with braid or other trim.

The larger the egg, the harder the shell and the more difficult it is to cut. Egg decorators say it's advisable to use a small drill when boring holes in a goose egg, and an ostrich egg may require a jeweler's saw.

APPLYING A HINGE

Get small brass hinges (with no holes) from a craft shop. Lay each hinge on the sticky side of a piece of cellophane tape, keeping the side to be glued up. Apply five-minute epoxy glue. Do not get it into the working part of hinge. Holding it by the tape, place hinge on the site (the opening you have cut). The tape will hold the hinge in place until the glue sets. When dry, discard the tape. Apply more glue over the ends of the hinges to secure them. Never put doors on eggs until the insides have been decorated. Hinges and doors are the last things to be added to the egg.

Aline Becker, who has a new book, *Heirloom Eggs* (1975), sent me the directions for the "Locket Egg," which she says is an easy one for beginners to make. "A personalized gift, such as this," she said, "will become a cherished heirloom."

LOCKET EGG

Lay a locket on a piece of paper and trace around it. Cut out and tape, top and bottom, in place on a small, fat blown goose egg (4¾ inches high). Draw around the paper pattern of the locket, then discard it.

Coat the eggshell over the line to be cut, and about 1 inch (2.5 cm.) to either side of it with Elmer's glue. Allow it to dry. Cut out the hole with nail scissors. For less breakage, cut counter-clockwise. Hold the egg to support it, but do not grasp it firmly. Cut around and around the hole, taking off a strip at a time. Try the locket on the hole for size. Trim until the hole is approximately the size of the locket.

111

Front of locket egg by Aline Becker.

112

Back of locket egg by Aline Becker.

Glue a ½-inch wide gold braid around the opening. Allow one edge of the braid to extend over the opening. Glue the locket over the hole, against the extended braid. Be sure you do not glue the locket shut or get glue into the locket's hinges.

Place the egg on an egg stand of your choice and draw a pencil line around the top of the stand. Glue braid around the penciled line. Now, glue the egg to the stand.

In back of the braid behind the locket, glue in order: gold cord, a strip of bias-cut white velvet, another gold cord, then more ½-inch braid, and a final gold cord.

The back of the egg is filled with a simple pattern of white and gold bugle beads, laid 3 one way, 3 another way. To fit the curve of the egg, a bead will occasionally be left out, or a matching recaille bead added. When completely dry, a coat of clear nail polish will seal the beads from the air, so they adhere more closely to the egg. The back may be varied by decoupaging a picture on it, or by making a hinged door to a lined compartment, inside the egg.

Glue a piece of jewelry—a pin or an earring—to the top as a finale, if desired.

You're now ready to fill the locket with photos.

Satisfactory egg stands may be made from various things. I find that the wire tops from champagne bottles, gilded with gold paint, make attractive stands and are pliable enough to fit various size eggs. This, like many other crafts, leaves much to the individual's ingenuity.

Aline Becker's book, *Heirloom Eggs*, may be ordered from the Treasure Chest, 87 Lewis Street, Phillipsburg, New Jersey 08865 for $4.95, plus 50 cents for postage and handling. If you're interested in advanced egg-decorating, get in touch with Kit Stansbury at the same address. She puts out a newsletter and several small booklets on the subject.

19

Dough Items

DOUGH breadbaskets are much more durable than one would suppose, and such fun to make that they appeal to all ages. They may be made in all sizes and colors but they're not edible. I've seen a basket that was forty years old and still in perfect condition. Shops that specialize in hand crafts may sell them for as much as $25.

BASKET

2 cups plain all-purpose flour (Make sure it's not self-rising.)
½ cup salt
¾ cup cold water
Gelatin molds (aluminum ones)
A metal or Pyrex pan the shape and size of the desired basket. For a
    small basket use aluminum gelatin molds.
Aluminum foil
Bread board or other surface for rolling
Rolling pin
Toothpicks (wooden) or tiny nails
Soft paint brush
Orange shellac or can of spray, clear finish
Lacquer (small bottles of model-car enamel may be substituted) of de-
    sired color

115

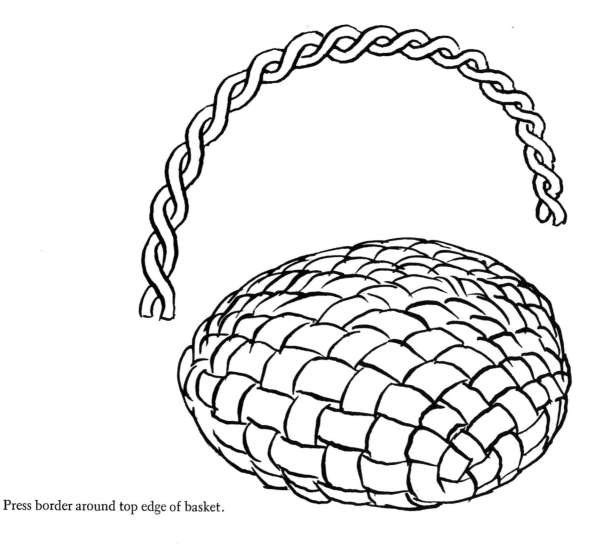

Press border around top edge of basket.

Combine flour, salt, and water, mixing thoroughly with your hands. Knead mixture on floured board or surface, until pliable. (Drops of water will work like glue in manipulating dough.)

Prepare the frame for your basket by covering the pan or mold with foil, making it snug to frame, and turning it under around the edges. Flour the board and rolling pin. Roll out as you would pie crust, making the dough long, if the strips are to be long to cover your frame. If you need longer strips than you have rolled, "glue" two strips together by wetting and pressing down. Dough should be about ¼ inch thick and strips about ¾ inches wide. Place the strips criss-cross on the foil frame, making sure the edges are neat. You may trim them as you would a pie crust. After the entire frame is covered with woven strips, secure them with toothpicks. Bake in a preheated oven at 325 degrees for 1½ hours. Test often as you would a pie crust; remember this should be much firmer.

116

Dough Items

After the dough is done, allow it to cool before removing the basket and foil from its frame. Handle gently. Turn basket upright and place it on a pie pan. Decorate the border by rolling or twisting the remaining dough around the edges of basket. Put back in oven for about 30 minutes, until edges are set firmly.

When cool, spray with clear finish or brush on orange shellac to seal all the pores and make the basket firmer. Make sure you cover all the sides of dough. When this first finish is dry, you may apply the first coat of color. About three coats should give the basket the permanency desired. After three coats of enamel or lacquer, the basket may be washed, if handled gently.

You may experiment with putting handles on and forming a flower border with the dough, if you like. If the dough becomes too dry for "working," a few drops of water will bring it back to desired consistency.

DOUGH BOY

2 cups flour	Pointed knife
¾ cup salt	Approximately 1 inch of fine wire
¾ cup water	Acrylic paint and varnish

Mix together 2 cups of flour, ¾ cup salt, and ¾ cup of water, depending on the humidity. Keep the unused dough covered to prevent drying.

Work on a piece of foil, and shape the trunk of the doll. Split the bottom for shorts and draw the suspenders and face with a pointed paring knife. Roll dough for legs and arms; twisting the ends of the leg dough for feet. Curve the arm dough so that it looks as if the hands are behind the back of the boy. Wire the limbs on with about 1 inch of fine wire, stuck into the body and the limb. Small wire may be inserted in the head for hanging, if desired. The boy's curly head is dough squeezed through a garlic press, scooped off the press with a knife, and applied to the doll.

Bake the doll on foil in a 250-degree oven for at least 1½ hours—until it sounds hollow when you tape it with a knife.

Cool the doll for 15 minutes and then decorate with acrylic paint. When dry, spray the doll front and back with acrylic varnish.

20

Handmade Christmas Tree Ornaments

CHRISTMAS is a family time when we build memories. At Christmas time, all over America, folks go home. The memories of those delicious kitchen smells, mixed with pine and cedar scents; the secretive atmosphere surrounding the gift wrappings and the fun of decorating the Christmas tree lingers with all of us into adult life. No matter how far away we may live, we long to go home on this most important holiday.

Decorating the tree has always been the highlight of Christmas at our house. It is important that every member of the family participate in this tradition. Homemade decorations are much more attractive than the ones we buy at the corner drugstores, and we are apt to become sentimental about the ones a member of the family makes.

Several years ago, when three light bulbs burned out within minutes of each other, I replaced them with exasperation. Surely there was something I could do with the burned-out bulbs! I placed them in my sewing basket, instead of the trash basket as I would normally do, thinking I would get back to them another day. Meanwhile, I kept thinking about them as I went about my work. Then I hit upon the idea of decorating them for the Christmas tree. After all, I reasoned, the old decorations were made of glass and china that had been hand-decorated. Why not these? After experimenting with some odds-and-ends, I came up with

118

four distinctly different ornaments; one for each member of the family. This is how I decorated them.

LIGHT BULB ORNAMENTS

Glue (use a cement such as Duro contact cement) a bottle cork to the screw-in part of the bulb. When firmly set, screw in a cup hook, for hanging the bulb on the tree.

Paint the bulb any color you desire with model-car enamel.

To make a jeweled ornament, brush over the bulb with cement (I used Elmer's cement) and roll it in sequins or crushed pearl buttons. Or you may place pearls or stones from broken costume jewelry in a circle around the bulb, as I did. There is no limit to the ways you can decorate the bulb, but it's important that you use a quick-setting cement, such as Elmer's.

Measure the neck of the bulb. Cut a piece of ribbon that length. Brush it with cement on one side first. Dip that side in "jewels" and let it dry.

Brush cement on the other side of ribbon and press it into place around the neck of the bulb.

Hang the ornament to dry thoroughly. A good drying place for all your bulbs can be made by screwing cup hooks into a heavy cardboard box (the packing kind) and hanging the ornament hooks on them. The box, turned on its side, protects the ornaments from dust and eliminates having to move them constantly from place to place. When they are thoroughly dry and the cement set, you may wrap them, as you would any other ornament, and store them away with your other Christmas decorations. Some of the jeweled ones I've made are so beautiful that I pack them separately in little boxes (you might use the carton the· original bulb came in) before putting them away, so there is no chance of their getting broken.

Doll Bulb Ornament

A little girl will love her very own doll ornament and it's so simple to make.

Use a larger cork for the doll than you did for the other ornaments. This is easily done by digging out the end of the cork, so that it will fit over the tip of the screw-in end of the bulb. I use cuticle scissors and cut out the cork, gradually, fitting it to the end of the bulb until the hole fits well.

Touch the end of the bulb with contact cement and put cement in

119

Three burned-out-light-bulb decorations. *Photo by Ross Chapple*

120

the hole in the cork, too. Place the cork over the end of the bulb and press down firmly. Wipe away any excess that may squeeze out. Hold it in your hand, pressing down, until the cement sets. The cork will be the face of your doll.

Either paint on a face, or do as I did, glue on a small face of a child or doll that you have clipped from a magazine.

Brush the "screw-in-part" of the bulb with cement. Wrap the bulb several times with bias tape or ribbon down to where it extends to its most bulbous part. This wrapping gives you a base to sew to for the neck and waists of the doll.

Select the materials for the doll's clothes. It may be fancy fabric or plain gingham. Measure around the wrapped section of the bulb and cut a piece of material adequate to cover that part. Wrap around the part and pull it together with stitches at the back of the doll.

Measure from the "waist" down to cover the entire bulb. Cut a piece of material that is wide and long enough to give fullness to the skirt. Stitch the seam on the back and gather it, leaving the needle and thread hanging until the skirt has been slipped over the head of the doll. When placed at the "waist," draw the thread tightly and top stitch several times to make sure that it holds. Do not cut the thread! Instead, start taking stitches around the doll between skirt and waist.

Measure from the bottom of the cork, over the top, and down the other side. Cut a piece of matching material about 1 inch wide, the length of the cork measurement. Stitch lace or binding around this piece and place it over the head of the cork, pull the ends to the back and stitch. This frames the face and makes a bonnet.

Trim the doll's outfit with ribbon or lace or whatever pleases you.

Screw the cup hook through the bonnet, which will secure it in place.

Bulbs may be hand-painted in many ways. You can write the name of a child or other member of the family on it. You may use a combination of pasted-on scenes from Christmas cards and paintings. Bulbs are fun to do and there is no loss if your first experiment doesn't turn out well. Who doesn't have a lot of burned-out light bulbs, when science has made a point of giving us bulbs with just so many "light-hours"?

Postage Stamp Bulb

Perhaps you have a stamp saver in the family. There are so many beautiful, decorative stamps being issued by the post office that it's easy to collect enough different stamps from your mail to cover an ordinary light bulb.

Paint the bulb a bright, Christmasy color.

Attach the cork and hook for hanging. (See above—"Light Bulb Ornaments.")

Cover the cork with large commemorative stamps. Work from the hanging end of the bulb to the more bulbous end, placing each stamp so that it meets its neighbor.

When the bulb is covered, and the contact cement is thoroughly dry, spray the bulb with quick-drying, clear shellac or varnish. Spray two or three times, making sure that the last coat is thoroughly dry before applying the next.

ALUMINUM-PIE-TIN ORNAMENTS

The aluminum pie tins that "store-bought pies" come in are ideal for making ornaments. The aluminum is more permanent than commercial foils and yet is thin enough so that sturdy, ordinary scissors will cut it. To make an angel, a star, or a Santa Claus, you'll need a pattern, a piece of carbon paper, and a good pair of scissors, preferably strong cuticle scissors. If you prefer, you may put your pattern on cardboard and cut it out; then trace it with pencil or pen onto the pie tin.

Cookie cutters make ideal patterns. They are easy to trace onto pie tins and come in a variety of shapes. Metal cookie cutters are easier to work with than plastic ones, but either will do. Put a thin paper over the pattern and trace. Then transfer the tracing (using carbon paper) to heavier paper or cardboard.

When decorating aluminum, you must use contact cement such as Duro, for water-soluble glues will not hold. Watercolors won't take either, but oil paints are fine. A needle and thread may be used, too, but the needle should be fairly large and strong to push through the aluminum tin.

WALNUT SHELL ORNAMENT

English walnut shells have been popular throughout history as the base for beautiful ornaments. These shells can be polished, painted, decorated, and hinged, then turned into little "boxes" for gifts of coins, jewels (especially rings), miniature photographs, and many other tiny things. There are three basic steps to preparing shells for craftwork:

• *Clean the shells out thoroughly.* If necessary, wash them with detergent and lay them out to dry. This helps to kill any eggs from termites or other bugs that may be inside. Walnuts should have been "cracked" carefully; try to preserve the two halves, when possible. One half of one shell will frequently match another half of another, however.

- *When dry, place on foiled cookie sheet in a preheated 200-degree oven.* After one minute, turn the oven off and let the shells stand until the oven cools.
- *Spray the shells with a sealer or paint with clear varnish.* Clear nail polish will do. When dry, match the shells so that when put back together, they appear whole. Wrap each one or place them in egg carton, two matched halves to an egg section.

Now you're ready to be artistic and imaginative. The inside of the shell can be painted or lined. Velvet ribbon makes a plush lining, although you may use anything you like. Brush on contact cement. When the inside of the walnut is covered, brush lightly over the back of material to be used with the cement, and press the material into place in the walnut. Press firmly with fingers until set. Trim surplus material around edges of the walnut. Gold braid or lace may be glued carefully around the rim of one side of walnut; allow it to extend out, so that the braid or lace will show as a frame around the nut when closed.

If you want to hinge the shell, do so before lining. To hinge, simply glue a small piece of material on the inside of each shell, making sure that the shell will close properly. You can experiment by taping the material first; then removing the tape and gluing it in the right position. Hinge first, so your lining will cover part of the hinge.

Gold paint is the most popular paint used on shells, although any color can be used. The natural shell is also pretty if sprayed several times with clear sealer or nail polish. The shell should be glossy.

Instead using material for lining, tiny pictures, cut from Christmas cards or magazines, may be glued to the inside of shell. To give a three-dimensional effect, glue the picture to a tiny piece of cardboard and attach them half-way inside the shell against a painted background. Experiment. There are so many things you can do. If you like walnut crafting, be on the lookout for all the tiny pictures and trims that adapt themselves to a tiny shell.

One of the prettiest ornaments, made from walnut shells, is the jeweled ball. It may be made with stones from a cheap piece of costume jewelry or from sequins that can be purchased at the dime store.

Attach a regular ornament hanger inside the shell. Glue it in place. Close the shell by gluing around the edges with cement.

Paint the whole thing gold, including the hanger attachment.

PASS IT ON

When dry, glue stones onto the shell, arranging them in an attractive pattern. If you haven't many stones, place them in the indented spaces of the shell, on the side that will face out from the tree. I like to cover the entire shell with sparkling stones. If you use sequins, brush cement over the surface of the shell, and roll it in "glitter." Depending on the materials you have to work with, this can be a work of art or just a pretty handmade decoration that enhances your tree and is unbreakable, long-lasting, and very apt to become a treasured heirloom for your family.

Making Christmas decorations should become a family project. It will encourage youngsters to use their imaginations and to feel that they are important in Christmas preparations. Who knows, you may discover an artistic talent in one of your children that you never knew existed. When walnuts first come on the market, usually in early fall, begin your Christmas planning. We used to have a contest that lasted for months. We offered a prize for the most attractively decorated walnut. If you do this, have some outsider do the judging. It's fun to give the walnuts numbers and lay them out for some occasion when friends or relatives gather; then have them vote on the walnut they like best. If the prize is awarded to a number, not a name, there can be no hard feelings among the family. Often this fires the determination to do better next year.

SEA SHELL ORNAMENTS

Making Christmas decorations from sea shells can offer a challenge to everyone who visits the beaches during the summer months. Some of our loveliest decorations have been made from the sea shells. Scrubbing a shell or sanding it down to the luster of mother-of-pearl is exciting. Looking for odd-shaped shells, that have the proper openings for tiny Christmas pictures, can turn an ordinary vacation into a treasure hunt.

- Select shells with a wide enough opening to house a Christmas picture.
- Scrub the shell with fine steel wool and detergent. If there are dark places, sand them lightly with fine sandpaper.
- Soak the shell overnight in a strong solution of liquid bleach and water. The solution should be about half and half.
- Dry shells thoroughly, in the sun if possible.

At the top of shell, work with a long, thin screw, turning it constantly, until a hole for hanging penetrates shell. If the shell is too thick for this process, cement a hanger hook to the top of the shell with Duro contact cement.

124

Decorated common sea shells done by James Hutchins. *Photo by Ross Chapple*

Arrange a small picture on the back of the shell and glue it there as you did on the walnut ornament, or glue it to cardboard and stand it away from the back, giving it a three-dimensional effect.

If the shell is dull, apply cement and sprinkle it with glitter.

If you're interested in decorating anything in the craft line, I suggest that you find a large shoe box that is wide enough to accommodate an envelope file style. Buy enough envelopes to fill the box and make tabs for each one. This way you can preserve your patterns, keep odd beads and stones from broken jewelry, save pretty cutout pictures you may want to use later, and store all of the other decorative materials you come across. Your materials will be in one place and labeled for easy finding.

A T.V. snack tray is an ideal working surface, and may be held in your lap. It is washable and will not be harmed if glue is spilled on it. An egg carton is ideal for holding your materials (jewels, sequins, corks, cup screws, etcetera) while working. A jar is handy for holding scissors, tweezers, and other tools needed for your work. An organized layout makes crafting more fun and much faster to do, because less time is spent looking for the things you need.

For most families, Christmas is an all-year-round affair. In summer, we think about gifts for various folks; we pay into Christmas savings clubs all year; and as early as October and November, some folks are wrapping presents for the upcoming holiday. Why not think about Christmas tree decorations the year round, too? No matter where your vacation takes you, be on the constant lookout for things that will enhance your tree. These happy family participations are the things that weave memories into heirlooms that we treasure for all our lives; they are the happy times that hold families together.

21

Shadow-Box or Frame Your Treasures

ONE of the most thoughtful things that parents can do for their children is preserve some of their most treasured possessions from childhood for the time when they are grown. With almost every child, there is a favorite toy, a trophy or some award or recognition that meant a lot to them. Little girls usually have one favorite doll that they loved above all the others. Cleaned up and dressed in her best clothes, such a doll will make a beautiful subject for shadow-boxing. Large antique shadow boxes with beautiful dolls sitting in miniature chairs or standing against a wall of pictures hang in the D.A.R. children's museum.

A friend of mine dressed her daughter's doll in an old-fashioned long dress, supported her with a wire frame, and framed her against a green-velvet background. The effect is so beautiful that it is the first thing you notice when you enter her living room. When my own daughter married, she packed her Betsy-Wetsy doll with her other things. "Who knows," she said, trying to hide her embarrassment at being caught wrapping it, "someday I may have a little girl who'll love her as I did."

Many boys receive merit badges from the Scouts or awards for some special skill. Instead of cluttering up drawers and taking a chance on their getting lost, why not frame them? It will please your son to know that you attached so much importance to his achievements.

PASS IT ON

When children are young, they're inclined to place little importance on taking care of their things. Nostalgia for old possessions is something indulged in by older people, such as their moms and dads, but the day will come when your children will thank you for thinking ahead and preserving their prized possessions from childhood. A ten-year-old may turn up his nose at a childish toy he cherished when he was five, but when he is in his teens, he'll show a burst of enthusiasm at having discovered it in a closet or stashed away in the attic.

Several years ago, I had a customer who collected old phonograph records. I saved all the early, thick records for him, thinking that he had an old Victrola to play them on but no, he framed them all. He'd used gold paper on the backgrounds, and hung them on the walls of his restaurant. If you have a few valuable, collector records, why not frame them and hang them on your walls? This way, they will never be broken or lost and you can pass them on to your children as a treasured heirloom.

The buttons from your husband's military service uniform, the medals he received while serving his country, or the special awards he may have received in his business make ideal objects to be framed. A little imagination and an inexpensive frame may preserve some part of your life that will mean a great deal to you and your children later on.

Nineteenth-century prints and engravings, cut from old books whose covers and bindings are tattered or missing altogether, make lovely pictures. These old books can be purchased for very little in secondhand book stores, for it is quite expensive to have a book rebound. Often the prints illustrating such books are beautiful and valuable. Copies of *Godey's Lady's Book*, *Harper's* and *Peterson* magazines (which came out yearly in book form) offer a wide variety of colorful prints. Old bird books have illustrations especially suitable for framing, too. Make sure that you keep the captions under the prints and engravings.

An old atlas with its many-colored maps provides good materials for framing. If there is a date on the maps, make sure it's preserved, because some very old maps are very valuable. Almost any young boy would love having framed maps hanging on his wall and most likely he will treasure them so much that he'll want to take them with him to college and later to his own house.

Pictures are an important part of your home's personality. The frame should suit the picture. A perfectly plain object should never be framed in an ornate frame. Art-supply stores carry a varied selection of framing materials; many that simply need to be put together. Dime-store frames are adequate for some objects, such as awards, phonograph records, or collections of things that need identical frames. Sometimes it's cheaper to buy a framed picture than a frame alone. Compare prices and consider that with many frames you must buy glass too. It's simple to remove a picture or print from a frame and insert your own, and often it's much less expensive. I prefer the cheaper, secondhand frames one might find in thrift shops, but unfinished frames can be stained and finished.

Any frame can be made into a shadow-box. There are several new super glues, such as Crazy Glue, on the market which will stick to almost anything with such force that they claim a man can be suspended in mid-air to a hat that has been glued to a beam. One must be very cautious working with these glues, for they will actually glue your fingers together. But a simple box frame—four pieces of pine wood cut to the size of the frame—can be attached to the frame with this glue and it will hold as well as screws or nails. You may use cardboard or plywood for the back. A table drawer, the right size to fit a frame, will work as well. In making a shadow-box, consider the depth needed for whatever you are going to frame. The backs may be wallpapered, covered with materials, or painted to give the proper background for your project.

Shadow-boxing your treasures can be fun, whether it be your child's christening dress or a collection of mounted butterflies. Decide what among your family's possessions will make the better heirloom and get busy and frame it. You might hide it until some future date and bring it out as a surprise. The family will love you for it.

22

Crafts for Children

CHILDREN should be taught, at an early age, to make things of lasting value. This teaches them to appreciate the time and thought that goes into the heirlooms we pass on to them.

PAPIER-MÂCHÉ PIGGY BANK

Many Chinese and Japanese antique wares were made of papier-mâché. The process is simple and may vary, for it is simply a meshing of crushed or stripped paper and glue or paste which becomes hard upon drying. I have selected a piggy bank as an interesting project for the beginner.

Materials

Select a base: either an oatmeal box, salt box, or a fat balloon which is
    longer than it is wide when blown up
3 double sheets of newspaper
1 cup of flour (any kind)
1 large cork for the bottom (This should be larger in size than a quarter.)
Bottles of model-car paint

Directions

If a balloon is used, blow it up to the size of the desired bank. Cut the newspaper into 1-inch strips. Mix the flour with water to a thin, paste

1. Strips dipped in paste and wrapped around balloon. 2. Finished figure.

consistency. Dip strips of paper into the paste and wrap them around your base, covering the base three or four times. Let the project dry overnight and, next day, repeat the wrapping process. Press two dabs into tent-like shapes for the pig's ears, and apply them in the proper place. Use four dabs for the feet and a bigger dab shaped into a snout. One small rolled strip will do for the curled tail. Again, let the project dry overnight. Now you're ready to paint the pig any color or combination of colors you desire. After the paint has dried thoroughly, cut the slit for dropping coins in. Cut a round hole in the bottom of the pig, make it the size of the cork. Fit the cork to the bottom and paint it the same color as the bank.

Every child loves a piggy bank and will enjoy it much more if he or she has participated in making his own. Let the children paint a happy face on the pig, using paints or magic markers.

COLLAGE

Collage is the art of gluing beads, beans, wire, or other raised materials to a surface. There are unlimited possibilities in collage for making plain boxes or plates into beautiful things. You might start a child off by

131

Floral collage
made with beans
and rice.

letting him collage a paper plate. Various colored beans are good materials to use or, perhaps, odd-shaped and colored rocks and stones that your child collected from your own yard. After he becomes proficient, let him graduate to decorating a china plate. This is a terrific way to discover his talents and it will encourage him to become creative.

For those interested in making jewelry or collage pieces, colorful, pretty materials to work with are toy marbles, which can still be bought by the bagful in most five-and-ten-cent stores. To crack the marbles so that they have a flat surface for gluing, drop the marbles into a frying pan and allow them to cook for several minutes over a medium flame on

132

top of the stove. Make sure they are heated through; then remove them and drop them into a bowl of ice water. They'll usually crack beautifully. If some don't, repeat the process.

Materials

Select your base: a paper plate, a box or tray, or almost anything that will
   be enhanced by decorating
Collect beads, beans, rocks, pieces of broken glass, or whatever you
   would like to work with
Elmer's cement for tin or glass, or Elmer's glue for paper
Container for glue
Tweezers

Directions

Draw a design lightly on your base with a pencil.

Pour glue into a lid or other container. Using tweezers, lightly dip beads, beans, or whatever you are using into the glue and place them around the outline of your design. You may fill in the whole design or simply outline it with your collage. On a black background, rice makes an attractive material for gluing, although it may be too difficult for children to work with. If you use beans or rice or other foodstuffs, it's wise to spray the finished project with a clear sealer or shellac to prevent bugs from getting into the food later. My sister once made a beautiful plate with a peacock done in colored beans; sometime later bugs (so tiny they appeared to be lice) began working inside the beans. The plate had to be destroyed to prevent the bugs from getting into other things in the house.

QUILLING

Quilling is an ancient art form that is being revived today. Nuns in the fifteenth century are believed to have originated the art by rolling narrow strips of paper around a quill pen. Hence, the name "quilling." Early examples of this work, often designed to look like carved ivory, may be seen in museums around the world. This is a simple craft that children will enjoy doing. The small coils may be shaped and set into almost any design to form a beautiful picture.

Materials

Strips of rag bond paper, cut ⅛ inch wide
Elmer's white glue
Knitting needle or corsage pin for coiling

133

PASS IT ON

Round toothpicks for opening coils
Tweezers
Wax paper (kitchen variety)
Egg cartons to hold coils until they're used
Plan or design which may be outlined on paper

Directions

Tight coil or circle. Wind strip of paper around pin or needle as tightly as possible. Slip pin or needle out and fasten coil with a drop of glue.

Looser coil. This is made by releasing the tight coil to the size desired, then gluing it. This is easily done by opening the coil carefully with a toothpick.

Shaped coil. To shape coils into flower petals, stars, or diamond shapes, loosen coils, as mentioned in the above paragraph, and pinch one end to make the petal, two ends to make a diamond and a star. Experiment with pinching to make all sorts of shapes, and after shaping, a drop of glue will hold them together. Experiment with looseness of coils and shapes that will enhance your design.

Lay wax paper on a flat surface and place your quills on it to form the design wanted. Tweezers are best for placing coils in the design. Dip a toothpick in glue and lightly glue the coils together. After a design has been finished, you can gently remove it from the wax paper to a permanent background of velvet, silk, or colored paper. The glue will not stick to wax paper.

THINGS YOU CAN DO WITH ROCKS

Odd-shaped rocks are fascinating. There are "rock hounds" who spend many hours looking for unusual rocks. In almost every city, there are enthusiasts who organize trips to mountains and countrysides to look for rocks. With a little imagination, the crafts-conscious person can turn an ordinary rock into a thing of beauty.

Large rocks can be decorated and used as doorstops; smaller rocks can be turned into paperweights; very small rocks can be used in various forms of collage. Rocks may be colored or decorated with appliqués or decoupage. James Hutchins, a telephone company executive in Raleigh, North Carolina, makes beautiful paper weights from rocks. Here are his instructions:

Materials

Unusual or pretty rocks that weigh about a pound. It's better if they
have a flat bottom

Rock that was decoupaged by James Hutchins, the deer being raised with putty. *Photo by Ross Chapple*

Stiff brush or steel-wool pad
Clear varnish or shellac
Picture to glue on rock
Contact cement
Piece of felt to fit bottom of rock

Directions

Scrub the rocks with a stiff brush or steel-wool pad. When thoroughly dry, cover the rock with clear varnish or shellac.

Cut out a suitable picture to apply. Raised pictures are especially pretty on rocks and can be done by applying putty to the back of picture for buildup. Coat with glue (over the putty) and press the rock gently down. Wipe off excess.

When picture is firmly set, cover the picture and entire rock with additional coats of clear varnish or shellac, making sure that each coat is thoroughly dry before applying the next.

Cut a piece of felt to fit the bottom of rock and glue it in place.

135

PASS IT ON

PAPER NEEDLEPOINT

Paper needlepoint or embroidery was very popular during the Victorian era and many bookmarks, mottoes, and samplers have been handed down through families. It is one of the easiest ways to teach a child to embroider and the results are as beautiful as those done on cloth. Many craft shops sell perforated paper for doing this work, but I have an easy way of making my own; by doing so, I can select any color paper I want.

This is how I prepare my paper.

Materials

Sheets of regular construction paper. Select several different colors.
Can of spray shellac in either colorless or the color of the paper used
Ice pick or corsage pin
Carbon paper or transfer
Embroidery thread and needle

Directions

Spray the entire sheet of paper you intend to use with shellac. It is good to spray several sheets while you're doing them, then you have them ready for future use.

When the sheets are dry, they'll have taken on a hard finish and are much less likely to tear when you perforate them.

Lightly mark off the sheet in 1-inch squares with a pencil.

Using an ice pick or corsage pin, perforate each square with either 16 holes or 12 holes. For fine work, 16 holes are better, but, for beginners, 12 holes are fine.

Trace a pattern onto the paper, either with a transfer or by tracing a picture from a magazine using carbon paper. For beginners, you might cut 1-inch strips from the sheet for a bookmark, using the same process. A small project will hold a child's interest longer.

Using cotton embroidery floss and a slender needle with a big eye, the child can do cross-stitching or satin-stitching, pushing the needle through the perforated holes. Lettering may be used instead of design for mottoes and these are easy to do, since you only count the holes for each letter. For a stronger bookmark, you can double the paper, matching the perforations.

In sewing on paper, always put the needle in one hole at a time. Never try to double up with extra stitches, because that will tear the paper. Put the needle in one hole and pull the thread all the way through before going to another hole. By counting holes, you'll always come up with an even design or letters.

136

Oatmeal box, painted
and decorated with
cut-outs from
magazine. *Photo by
Ross Chapple*

137

Putting Designs on Tin Cans

Any tin can that has a paper label on it can be made into an unusual vase or flower pot. When I visited a friend recently and admired a pretty vase on her desk, she told me how she had made it.

Materials

1 tall 46-ounce grapefruit-drink can
1 paper doily
Ice pick

Directions

Neatly remove the top from a tall can to form the base. Remove the label and wash the can out. Then refill the can with water to the top and place it in the freezer.

When the can of water is thoroughly frozen, remove it from the freezer and surround the can with the doily, taping it where it meets.

With an ice pick, follow the design on the doily by punching holes through the doily holes into the can. The ice inside the can prevents the can from bending. When you have followed the pattern of the doily all around the can, remove the doily and empty out the ice. The effect is beautiful and this size can holds a quart jar well, as a liner, to hold water so the can may be used as a flower vase. Without the liner, the can may be used as a flower planter, the design holes offer drainage for the plants.

Decorate All Kinds of Boxes

Disposable boxes, such as oatmeal, salt, cracker, or potato-chip boxes are ideal for starting a child out in craft projects. Use a glue or paste suitable for the child's age, and let him paste magazine pictures, cloth pictures, yarn, sea shells, and any other craft materials available on the box. Encourage your child to be creative. There is nothing lost if his first attempts are not attractive. These type boxes with their covers make nice storage containers for crayons, pencils, clips, sewing materials, and other things that clutter a drawer. Often the results are pretty enough to be used as gifts or gift containers.

23

Where to Sell Your Crafts and Buy Supplies

OFTEN, when we start making our own heirlooms, we become so enthusiastic with one craft or another that we are apt to make far more than we can use or need ourselves. It's good to know that there are craft shops all over the country eager to sell handmade crafts and that our hobbies may become profitable as well as fulfilling.

Most craft shops specialize in homemade items but some sell antiques, baked goods, candy, and other things as well. It's of the utmost importance that you never send your items to any shop without first writing to it and getting permission to do so. Some shops will not carry the same items from two or more different people, because of the competition involved. If a shop handles your quilts, they may not want to take someone else's until the ones they have are sold. There is usually a 20 to 30 percent commission charge, which is deducted when the item is sold. When you write to a shop, ask for details and tell them what your specialty is. Then, by all means, insure your items, when you have made arrangements to have a shop sell them for you.

HOW TO SELL YOUR CRAFTS

Leta Clark, author of *How To Make Money With Your Crafts*, offers very good advice for those who wish to sell their crafts to retail stores in their areas. After you have called for an appointment to show the buyer your wares, tag each item with the following information:

139

PASS IT ON

- Label each sample with a number. Show the buyer your most attractive work.
- Show the size on the label. If the craft is to fit a certain size person or pillow, make sure you are right on marking the label.
- List all the shades or colors the item comes in. If it is red, say so. Don't think up fancy names like "flaming" something or other.
- Washing or cleaning instructions should be included.
- List wholesale prices by item, pair, or dozen. Never suggest a retail price to the buyer. He knows his business better than you do.
- State minimum orders. It's not always profitable to do one of a kind.
- Before you send or take items to a store to fill an order, have the order signed by the buyer and a cutoff date for delivery. No matter how firm the order may seem verbally, do not start work until the order is signed.

There may be shops in your own town or city that will sell on consignment, but mail-order consignment shops (especially the ones I will list here) are specialty craft shops and are apt to get a great deal more for your items than a general consignment shop.

SHOPS THAT SELL CRAFTS ON CONSIGNMENT

Appalachian Spring
1655 Wisconsin Avenue, N.W.
Washington, DC 20007

Chestnut Hill Community Center
8419 Germantown Avenue
Philadelphia, PA 19118

The Country Store
113 W. Franklin Street
Chapel Hill, NC 27514

Craftsmen Unlimited, Inc.
16 Main Street
Bedford Hills, NY 10507

Dedham Woman's Exchange, Inc.
445 Washington Street
Dedham, MA 02026

The Depot
217 First Street
Hohokus, NJ 07423

The Elder Craftsmen Showcase
850 Lexington Avenue
New York, NY 10021

Fairfield Woman's Exchange, Inc.
332 Pequot Road
Southport, CT 06490

Family Arts Exchange
5807 N. 7th Street
Phoenix, AZ 85014

Greenwich Exchange for
    Woman's Work, Inc.
28 Sherwood Place
Greenwich, CT 06830

The Hay Scales Exchange Inc.
2 Johnson Street
North Andover Center, MA 01845

The Hen House
4816 Tippecanoe Drive
Evansville, IN 47715

Heritage Village Woman's
 Exchange
Southbury, CT 06488

The Hunterdon Exchange
155 Main Street
Flemington, NJ 08822

Ladies Depository Association of
 Philadelphia
109 South 18th Street
Philadelphia, PA 19103

Litchfield Exchange for Woman's
 Work, Inc.
Cobble Court
Litchfield, CT 06759

The Little Turtle Woman's
 Exchange
Time Corner Shopping Center
Fort Wayne, IN 46804

The Mulberry Gallery
28 Court Street
Westfield, MA 01085

Newark Exchange for Woman's
 Work
32 Halsey Street
Newark, NJ 07102

New York Exchange for Woman's
 Work, Inc.
541 Madison Avenue
New York, NY 10022

Old Town Hall Exchange
Lincoln Center, MA 01773

The Old York Road Woman's
 Exchange
429 Johnson Street
Jenkintown, PA 19046

St. Michael's Woman's Exchange
5 Highland Park Village
Dallas, TX 75205

Sandhills Woman's Exchange
Pinehurst, NC 28374

The Sassy Cat
88 North Main Street
Chagrin Falls, OH 44022

Scarsdale Woman's Exchange,
 Inc.
33 Harwood Court
Scarsdale, NY 10583

The Stamford Woman's
 Exchange
45 Prospect Street
Stamford, CT 06901

Unique Corner—The Woman's
 Exchange of Athens
Taylor-Grady House
634 Prince Avenue
Athens, GA 30601

The Village Exchange
De Forest & Woodland Avenues
Summit, NJ 07901

The Woman's Exchange
993A Farmington Avenue
West Hartford, CT 06107

The Woman's Exchange
36 Exchange Street
Portland, ME 04111

The Woman's Exchange
3507 Michigan Avenue
Cincinnati, OH 45208

Woman's Exchange of Brooklyn,
 Inc.
76 Montague Street
Brooklyn, NY 11201

The Woman's Exchange of
 Memphis, Inc.
88 Racine Street
Memphis, TN 38111

PASS IT ON

Woman's Exchange of
 Monmouth County
32 Church Street
Little Silver, NJ 07739

The Woman's Exchange of
 Reading, Inc.
720 Penn Avenue
West Reading, PA 19602

Woman's Exchange Special Ties
 of Tucson
4215 North Campbell
Tucson, AZ 85719

The Woman's Exchange of West
 Chester

10 South Church Street
West Chester, PA 19380

The Woman's Exchange of
 Yardley
47 West Afton Avenue
Yardley, PA 19077

Woman's Industrial Exchange
541 Penn Avenue
Pittsburgh, PA 15222

Woman's Industrial Exchange
333 North Charles Street
Baltimore, MD 21201

Of course, there are many more shops than the ones listed here. I suggest that you look under "Arts and Crafts" in the yellow pages of your phone book for those in your area.

Where to Get Mail-Order Craft Supplies

From time to time, every person doing crafts will need certain supplies not always available in their local stores, and for that reason I have compiled a list of concerns that will supply catalogs and accept mail orders. Some of the catalogs are free and some charge a small fee, but most request a self-addressed, stamped envelope for even the free catalogs. This extensive list was compiled by Kit Stansbury, who is Director of the Egg-Crafters. Mrs. Stansbury has been kind enough to give me permission to use it. I have also added a few other addresses to her list.

A 'n L's Hobbicraft, Inc.
50 Broadway
Asheville, NC 28807
(Catalog, $1.00)
All crafts including egging supplies

Aiko's Art Materials Import
714 North Wabash Avenue
Chicago, IL 60611
Imported Japanese art supplies

American Handicrafts
Fort Worth, TX 76110
(Catalog, free)
General crafts

Ann & Gloria's Chelsea Shop
127 Grand Street
Goshen, NY 10924
(Catalog, 50¢)
Features egg and boutique supplies

142

P.S. Andrews Co.
603 South Main Street
St. Charles, MO 63301
(124-page catalog, $2.00)
Arts & crafts supplies

Anita of California
10950 Longford Street
Lakeview Terrace, CA 91342
(Catalog, 25¢)
China painting supplies

Barbara's Original Dolls
Box 2805
Valdesta, GA 31601
(List, 20¢ and self-addressed,
stamped envelope)
*Dolls of matchsticks, toothpicks
and corsage pins*

Bernier Studio
Route 25
Wentworth Village, NH 03282
(Self-addressed, stamped envelope
for price list)
Stained-glass supplies

Dorothy Biddle Service
Dept. TC-RE
Hawthorne, NY 10532
(Catalog, 10¢)
Everything for flower arranging

Mrs. Gustave Birk
Route 1, Box 164
Frenchtown, NJ 08825
($2.00, plus 25¢ postage)
*Doll, all original, made from
cotton-tip swab*

Dick Blick
P.O. Box 1267
Galesburg, IL 61401
(Catalog available)
All craft supplies and materials

Bottle Crafts
10309 Vassar Avenue
Chatsworth, CA 01311
(Self-addressed, stamped envelope
for details)
Bottle cutter

Boutique Trims
P.O. Box 205
South Lyon, MI 48178
(Catalog, $1.00)
Specializes in egg supplies

Boxwood Crafters
1141 Commercial Drive
Lexington, KY 40505
(Colorful brochure, free)
*18 lamp styles, finished &
unfinished*

Boycan Crafts
Sharon, PA 16146
(Catalog, 50¢)
Crafts supplies

Brookstone Company
16 Brookstone Building
Peterborough, NH 03458
(Catalog available)
"Hard to find tools" & other items

W. Atlee Burpee Company
5175 Burpee Building
Warminster, PA 18974
(Free seed catalogs)

Candle Kitchen
27 South Union Avenue
Cranford, NJ 07016
(Catalog, 35¢)
Candle-making supplies

The Candle Mill
East Arlington, VT 05252
(Catalog)
Candle supplies & gift items

PASS IT ON

Chestnut Hill Studio, Ltd.
Box 38
Churchville, NY 14428
Mail order only
(Catalog, $1.50)
Handmade miniatures & furniture

Albert Constantine & Son, Inc.
2050 Eastchester Road
Bronx, NY 10461
(Catalog, 50¢)
All supplies for woodworking

Hallie Copeland
Box 634
Morro Bay, CA 93442
(Self-addressed, stamped envelope
for price list)
Bread dough miniatures

Country Crafts
Route 208
Maybrook, NY 12543
(Catalog, $1.00)
*Miniatures, egg stands, hinges,
glitter, rare braids, jewels, beads,
etcetera*

The Craft Corner
P.O. Box 5754
Augusta, GA 30906
(Price list 10¢ plus self-addressed,
stamped envelope)
*Beads, candlecraft supplies,
boutique items, etcetera*

Craftex
P.O. Box 9591
Seattle, WA 08119
(Catalog, $1.00)
Jewelry & lapidary supplies

Crafty's Backroom
R.D. #1, Box 7

Augusta, NJ 07882
(Catalog, $1.00)
Eggery & boutique supplies

Crowe & Coulter
Box 484TC
Cherokee, NC 28719
(Self-addressed, stamped envelope
for brochure)
Woodcarving & weaving supplies

Creative Craft House
910 St. Vincent Avenue
Santa Barbara, CA 93101
(10¢ stamp for money-making idea
craft booklet; 56-page catalog, 35¢)
Miniatures & crafts supplies

Creative Hands Co., Inc.
P.O. Box 11602
or
4146 Library Road
Pittsburgh, PA 15234
(Catalog)
All crafts and supplies

Creative Spoolcraft
252 South Middletown Road
Pearl River, NY 10965
(Catalog, 60¢)
*Kits and supplies for spool orna-
ments*

Decorative Supply Center, Inc.
P.O. Box 2898
or
926 West Second
Wichita, KS 67201
(Catalog)
*Artist's supplies, metal, wood,
hardware, etcetera*

Caroline Dellaventura
215 Bryson Avenue
Staten Island, NY 10314
Styrofoam ball marker

144

Derby Lane Shell Center
10515 Gandy Boulevard
St. Petersburg, FL 33702
(Catalog, 50¢)

Diamond A. Studio
2516 Northwest 27th Avenue
Portland, OR 97212
(Price list available)
Paints and designs

The Dollhouse Factory
812 Lennox Court
Sunnyvale, CA 94087
(Catalog, 50¢)
Miniature dollhouse furnishings

The Dollhouse Factory
Box 456—157 Main Street
Lebanon, NJ 08833
(Catalog available)
Dollhouse accessories

Double "R" Gift Shop
R.F.D. 1, Route 302
Lisbon, NH 03585
(Catalog, 25¢)
*Everything in the bead-making
line*

Edabub's Dollhouse
R.D. 1, Box 84B
Great Barrington, MA 01230
(Catalog, 50¢)
*Dolls in costume, doll supplies,
dollhouse furniture, etcetera*

The Egg Shell
P.O. Box F
South Lyon, MI 48178
(Information, 25¢)
Egg marker, stands, etcetera

The Egg Stand
R.D. 1, Box 142

East Greenville, PA 18041
*Miniatures, ceramic, bisque,
etcetera*

The Enchanted Doll House
Manchester Center, VT 05255
(Catalog, $1.00)
*Dollhouses, miniature furniture &
accessories*

Enchanted Toy Shop
23812 Lorain Road
North Olmsted OH 44070
(Catalog, 75¢)
*Dollhouses, furniture, miniatures
(over 500 items, scale 1 inch = 1
foot)*

Fantasy Creations
11 Birchwood Road
Danville, NJ 07834
(Catalog, 25¢)
Bread dough miniatures

C. Ference
P.O. Box 295
Saline, MI 48176
(Self-addressed, stamped envelope
for information)
Ukrainian egg art supplies

Wilma Ference
686A South Main Street
Phillipsburg, NJ 08865
(Self-addressed, stamped envelope
for list)
*Handmade miniatures of balsa
wood*

Betty Fielding
123 Donovan Avenue
Mogadore, OH 44260
*Miniature figures handmade and
painted*

145

PASS IT ON

Florida Supply House, Inc.
P.O. Box 847
Bradenton, FL 33507
(Catalog free)
Shell and jewelry findings

Annie P. Forbes
304 Adams Street
Milton, MA 02186
*New Ashford, New Zealand
spinning wheels available*

Gail's Decorative Arts Studio
P.O. Box 696
Olympia Station
Miami, FL 33165
(Catalog, $1.00)
Eggery and boutique supplies

The Golden Egg
210 Crain Highway
D South
Seven Run Building
Millersville, MD 21108
Blown eggs and egg stands

Connie Gordon, Inc.
530 Lincoln Road
Miami Beach, FL 33139
(Self-addressed, stamped
envelope)
Art supplies and instructions

Mary A. Hanusey
244 West Girard Avenue
Philadelphia, PA 19123
*All necessary supplies for Pysanky/
Ukrainian eggs*

Joseph Harris Company, Inc.
56 Moreton Farm
Rochester, NY 14624
(Free seed catalogs)

Betty Hartung
R.D. 2–Box 218
Phillipsburg, NJ 08865
(Write for price list)
*Wedding dolls made to order,
also Barbie and Ken outfits*

Hobbycraft
1020 South Wells
Reno, NV 89502
(Miniature list, 25¢)
All crafts available

Holiday Craft
9 Main Street
Sparta, NJ 07871
(Design folio, catalog, $1.00)
*Plastic shapes for decor and varied
egging and boutique supplies*

Holiday Handicrafts, Inc.
P.O. Box 470
Winsted, CT 06098
(Free catalog)
*General hobby and craft kits and
supplies*

House of Rachel
P.O. Box 38406
Dallas, TX 75238
(Price list, 25¢)
*Specializing in eggery supplies and
Jane's frosting*

Howe Studio—Arts & Crafts
P.O. Box 178
Lake Havasu City, AZ 86403
(Brochure, 25¢)
*Ceramic eggs, stands, and minia-
tures to decorate*

Marion Howes
23421 Woodfield Road
Gaithersburg, MD
Custom-made dollhouses

Betty James Originals
Box 774K
Severna Park, MD 21146
(Price list, 25¢)
Rag doll patterns (original)

Jeane's
9 Church Street
Fairhope, AL 36532
(Catalog with instructions, $2.00)
Decoupage supplies

Lee Wards
P.O. Box 206
Elgin, IL 60120
(Catalog free)
Craft and needlecraft supplies

Leisure Craft
Box 743
Mendota, MN 55150
(Catalog, 25¢—Refundable)
Metallic braids in antique and bright finish made in West Germany and Austria

Lilliput House
228 15th Street Northwest
Massillon, OH 44646
(Self-addressed, stamped envelope for price list)
Specializes in handmade needlework in miniature, scale 1 inch = 1 foot)

Liz's Little Shop
P.O. Box 246
Barlow, KY 42024
(Price list, 25¢)
Mini bread dough fruits, garden produce, etcetera, dollhouses and furniture

Macramé Studio
3001 Indianola Avenue
Columbus, OH 43202
Macramé, beads and looms

Maid of Scandinavia Company
3245 Raleigh Avenue
Minneapolis, MN 55416
Cake decor items and craft materials

Mari Mountgarden
Room 78, 320 Elwood Avenue
Oakland, CA 94610
Pysanky egg kits, needlepoint kits

Microbus
534 Red Haw Road
Dayton, OH 45405
Miniature dishes, toys, silver, glass, etcetera, 1 inch = 1 foot scale

Miki's House, Inc.
Box 84
Carmel, IN 46032
(Self-addressed, stamped envelope for information)
The Embroidered Egg and other egg kits

Mildred's Eggurey Art & Craft
East Presidio Road
Phoenix, AZ 85022
Pen and ink designs

Mini Crafts
6610 Melshore Drive
Mentor, OH 44060
(Catalog, $1.00, including instructions)
Eggery supplies, supplies for mini gardens

Mother Goose
Windswept Estates

Route 3, #37 Charlay
Imperian, MO 63052
(Self-addressed stamped envelope
for price list)
*Copyrighted patterns for original
dolls—all kinds*

National Artcraft Supply Co.
12217 Euclid Avenue
Cleveland, OH 44106
(Catalog, $1.00)
Jewelry findings, stones, etcetera

George W. Park Seed Company,
Inc.
98 Cokesbury Road
Greenwood, SC 29647
(Free seed catalog)

The Pink Sleigh
Oldwick Road, Route 523
P.O. Box 35
Oldwick, NJ 08858
(Catalog, 50¢)
*Eggery and boutique supplies and
kits*

Posy Patch Originals
Box 38223, Capitol Hill Station
Atlanta, GA 20334
(Color brochure, 25¢)
*Miniature flowers of bread dough
1 inch = 1 foot scale*

The Putter Shop
Box 66
Congers, NY 10920
(21-page brochure, 70¢)
*Eggery and boutique supplies, also
Christmas ornament kits*

Geraldine S. Rarick Studio, Inc.
1407 Main Street
Longmont, CO 80501

(Pictorial brochure, 25¢)
*Designs for china painting and
other purposes*

Roblyn's Crafts
462 Foothill Boulevard
La Canada, CA 91011
(Catalog, 25¢)
Complete line of eggery supplies

Rock Mountain Farm
Box 167
Mosier, OR 97040
(Price list, 25¢)
Eggery supplies

Sandy's Crafts
308 Pope Street
Bridgewater, VA 22812
(Catalog, $1.00)
*General egg supplies and egg lamp
kits*

Sax Arts & Crafts
207 North Milwaukee Street
Milwaukee, WI 53202
(Large catalog, $1.00)
All arts and crafts supplies

Eleanor Scholz
410A Main Street
Boonton, NY 07005
*Dollhouse miniatures and
accessories*

Sy Schweitzer & Co., Inc.
Box 431
West Greenwich, RI 02818
(Catalog, 50¢; 1st class & Canada
80¢)
Jewelry-making supplies

Sears, Roebuck Company
(Request craft catalog from
nearest mail-order source or store)
All crafts and kits

Stokes Seeds, Inc.
Box 548
Buffalo, NY 14240
(150-page seed catalog)

Seedway, Inc.
P.O. Box 18124
Hall, NY 14463
(Free seed catalog)

Supreme Handicrafts
Box 395
Sioux Falls, SD 57101
(Catalog, 25¢)
All crafts

Surma Book & Music Company, Inc.
11 East 7th Street
New York, NY 10003
(Self-addressed, stamped envelope for price list)
All materials for Ukrainian egg art

W. Spencer, Inc.
446 Fore Street
Portland, ME 04111
(Catalog, retail 50¢. If in business, request wholesale catalog)
Candle-crafting supplies

Takashimaya, Inc.
401 Old Country Road
Carle Place, NY 11514
(Literature available)
Origami, Oshibana, Sumie art material

Taylor House
Corner Bench and Perry Streets
Galena, IL 61036
(Catalog, 75¢)
Egger and boutique supplies

Terminal Hobby Shop
4054 North 34th Street
Milwaukee, WI 53216
(Catalog, $3.00)
H.O. Catalog includes miniatures

The Tree House
3 Boar Court
Suffern, NY 10901
(Brochure, 25¢)
Christmas ornaments

Tree Toys
P.O. Box 492
Hindsdale, IL 60521
Quilling supplies

Triarco Arts & Crafts
3201 North Kimball
Chicago, IL 60618
(Catalog available)

Village Miniatures
Route 3, Box 289M
Chesterfield, MO 63017
(Catalog, $1.00)
Miniatures

Wilton Enterprises, Inc.
833 West 115th Street
Chicago, IL 60643
(Catalog, $1.50)
Cake decorating supplies and miniatures

Gene Woods Original Designs
126 East Sunset Road
San Antonio, TX 78209
(Self-addressed, stamped envelope for price lists)
Design patterns, also cutout kits

World Arts
503 North Broad
Wilmington, CA 90744

PASS IT ON

(Self-addressed, stamped envelope for information)
Custom needlepoint canvas
(*photo reproduced on canvas for you to complete*)

Wood Works
Junction Road
Brookfield Center, CT 06805
(Self-addressed envelope for brochure)

June Zimonick's Studio
840 Cook Street, Box 113

DePere, WI 54115
(Catalog, $2.00)
Egg, ornament and boutique kits and supplies

Zymex
900 West Los Vallecitos
San Marcos, CA 92069
(3 catalogs available: #74G Jewelry Making Supplies, $1.00; #74C Craft Catalog, $1.00; Needlework catalog, 50¢)

Index

Allen, James, 15
ancestry, tracing, 26–30
apple doll, 100–102
appliqués, 31, 41, 43, 46, 77–78
arranging pressed flowers, 59–60
autographs: collecting, 12–15, 24; political, 13–15; preserving, 15

basket, dough, 115–117
Becker, Aline, 111, 114
bed, dollhouse, 96, 98
Bible, family, 11, 27
Bicentennial: scrapbook, 9; quilt, 37
boxes: decorating, 138; lining with newsprint, 10–11
braided rug, 50–53

cards, collecting, 12–15
carry all, 36
catalogs, craft, 142–150
chair, dollhouse, 96, 99
children's crafts, 130–138
chili, 24
Chinese vase, potichomania, 74

Christmas tree ornaments, 118–126
Clark, Leta, 140
clock, dollhouse: decorator's 99; grandfather, 98
clothespin doll, 108
coat of arms, 26
collage, 131–133
collecting: autographs, 12–15, 24; flowers, 57; greeting cards, 12–15, 24
cookbooks: famous people, 24; handmade, 17, 22, 23; personal, 16–25
cornhusk doll, 102–106
coverlets, 38–46
Crawford, Marguerite Cain, 103
cutouts, gluing to glass, 73–75

Dankel, Glenroy, 109
decorations: on boxes and cans, 138; Christmas, 118–126; on eggshells, 110; on lampshades, 9, 60
decoupage, 65–72; sampler, 48
diorama, egg, 110–111

doll bulb-ornament, 119–121
dollhouse furniture, 89–99
dollhouses, 89–99
dolls: apple, 100–102; bulb-ornament, 119–121; clothespin, 108; cornhusk, 102–103; dough, 117; "me," 106–107
dough items, 115–117
dried-flower arrangements, 62–64
drying: eggshells, 110; flowers, 62–64

egg-crafting, 109–114; emptying eggshells, 110
Eisenhower, Mrs. John, 54
Elizabeth Husch, 17, 20–21
embroidery: family tree, 29–30; pressed flower sampler, 47–49; quilt, 34–35

Fabergé, Peter Carl, 109
family coverlet, 45–46
family crests, 26
family history: notebook, 28; quilt, 36–37

151

Index

family tree: embroidered or painted, 29–30; tracing, 26–30
Fitzgerald, F. Scott, 89
Five-Minute Cookies, 23–24
Flacklam, Margaret, 103
floors, dollhouse, 95
flower press, 57–58
flowers, drying, 62–64: air, 62–63; with borax, 63–64; with glycerine, 64
flowers, pressed, 54–60: arranging, 59–60; collecting, 57; pressing, 58–59; sampler, 47–49; storing, 59; tips, 60
framing, 11, 127–129
furniture, dollhouse, 89–99

glass, gluing cutouts to, 73–75
grandfather clock, dollhouse, 98
greeting cards, collecting, 12–15

hand design coverlet, 45–46
hanging shelf, whittled, 86–88
Happy-Face Coverlet, 41–43
headlines, historic, 7, 11
Howes, Marion, 91
Humelsine, Carl, 24
Husch, Elizabeth, 17, 20–21
Hutchins, James, 134

Johnson, Lyndon, 24

Kalama, Mealii, 31
Kennedy: autographs, 13; scrapbook, 9
knick-knacks, dollhouse, 99

lamp bases, potichomania, 75
lampshades: decorating, 60; newsprint, 9
light bulb ornaments, 119–122
locket egg, 111, 114
Lutyens, Edwin, 89

Marie Antoinette, 65
"me doll," 106–108

memory coverlet, 43–45
miniature furniture, 89–99
Moore, Colleen, 89

National Archives, 8, 28
needlepoint, paper, 136
Newman, Thelma, 72
newspapers: collecting, 3–11; lampshade, 9; headline scrapbook, 9; storing and preserving, 8; tray, 10; trunklining with, 10–11
newspaper scrapbook, 9
Nixon, Richard M., 7, 9
Null, Ralph, 62

O'Neil, Sunny, 54, 57, 59
ornaments: Christmas, 118–126; egg-crafted, 109–114

painting: on eggs, 110; on velvet, 76–77; on wood, 79–82
paper weights, rock, 134–135
papier-mâché piggy bank, 130–131
patchwork quilts, 36–37
penny pouf quilt, 31–34
Phibbs, Patricia, 103
pie-tin ornaments, 122
piggy bank, papier-mâché, 130–131
postage-stamp bulb, 121–122
potichomania, 73–75
pouf coverlet, 38–41
pressed flowers, 54–60: and embroidery sampler, 47–49

Queen Mary, 89
quilling, 133–134
quilts, handmade, 3, 6, 31–37

recipes, 16–25: Elizabeth Husch's Apple Strudel, 20–21; Kentucky Whiskey Cake,

22–23; Lyndon Johnson's Pedernales River Chili, 24; Five-Minute Cookies, 23–24
Rockefeller, Nelson, 13
rocker, whittled, 84–86
rocks, 134–135
rug, braided, 50–53

samplers, 47–49
scrapbooks, 5, 9
sea shell ornaments, 124–126
selling your crafts, 139–142
shelf, hanging, whittled, 86–88
shadow-boxes, 64, 127–129
sofa, dollhouse, 95–96
Sophie Mae's Peanut Butter, 16–17
Stansbury, Kit, 109, 114, 142
stew, football, 22
storing: flowers, 59; newspapers, 8
storybook quilt, 34
shops, craft, 139–150
supplies, craft, 142–150

tables, dollhouse, 99
tester bed, dollhouse, 96, 98
tin can designs, 138
tray, newsprint, 10
tree ornaments, 118–126
trunks, lining, 10–11

Ukranian eggs, 109

vanity, dollhouse, 99
velvet painting, 76–77

walls, dollhouse, 95
walnut shell ornament, 122–124
Welk, Lawrence, 13
Whiskey Cake, 22–23
Winnie the Pooh quilt, 34
Wood: painting on, 79–82; whittling, 83–88